Contents

Lighten our darkness...

Over the last couple of years or so, all of us, to different degrees, have experienced darkness. As I write, there are uncertain glimmers of light. But, as always, the darkness of our needy world still asks its difficult questions. Our hope – as for God's people in Israel and New Testament Christians – is in Jesus, the Light of the World.

First in this *Daily Bread*, we read of Jesus' great ancestor, King David (2 Samuel). Distant historically, but his life and times have similarities to our own. Look out for threads of light that weave through this story. Later on, we come to the uncomfortable words of the prophet Jeremiah. God's justice and judgement for those who persistently prefer evil are terrible, but remember that such reckoning also brings good news. And for all God's people, Jeremiah's message brings promise of light and renewed relationship with God (Jeremiah 31:33,34).

In Luke's Gospel we meet 'the Light' himself. As Jesus heads for Jerusalem, we discover our God who knows well the shadows of this world, but keeps focused on the joy of heaven.

As Terry Clutterham writes, Jesus is not unsettled by life's challenges but remains steady, sight fixed on God's purposes. In his letter to the Philippians, St Paul celebrates the amazing truth of the Christmas story – Jesus, found 'in human likeness', looking forward to heavenly glory (Philippians 2:9–11).

So, let's come to God's Word now. As we read, may Jesus lighten our darkness. As we live, may we 'shine ... like stars ... as [we] hold firmly to the word of life' (Philippians 2:15,16).

'Tricia and Emlyn Williams
Editors

Daily Bread toolbox

Tricia & Emlyn Williams worked with Scripture Union for many years. Emlyn led Schools ministry, then worked with SU International. Tricia was also part of the Schools team and later worked for SU Publishing, developing, writing and editing Bible resources. Having recently completed research in the area of faith and dementia, she continues with writing and editing faith resources. Retired from his role as discipleship pastor in a local church, Emlyn now continues his writing and talking-with-people ministries.

WAY IN

This page introduces both the notes and the writer. It sets the scene and tells you what you need to know to get into each series.

A DAY'S NOTE

The notes for each day include five key elements: *Prepare, Read* (the Bible passage for the day), *Explore, Respond* and *Bible in a year.* These are intended to provide a helpful way of meeting God in his Word.

PREPARE

Prepare yourself to meet with God and pray that the Holy Spirit will help you to understand and respond to what you read.

READ

Read the Bible passage, taking time to absorb and simply enjoy it. A verse or two from the Bible text is usually included on each page, but it's important to read the whole passage.

EXPLORE

Explore the meaning of the passage, listening for what God may be saying to you. Before you read the comment, ask yourself: what is the main point of this passage? What is God showing me about himself or about my life? Is there a promise or a command, a warning or example to take special notice of?

RESPOND

Respond to what God has shown you in the passage in worship and pray for yourself and others. Decide how to share your discoveries with others.

BIBLE IN A YEAR

If your aim is to know God and his Word more deeply, why not follow this plan and read the whole Bible in one year?

Back to the beach!

How we missed having holidays and missions in person during the pandemic! But thanks to your faithful support and with the determined efforts of many amazing volunteers, in summer 2021 things started returning to normal. And hundreds of children and young people encountered the God who loves them.

SU Mission Enabler Toby Chant, together with others from the South West Regional Team, took on running Polzeath Family Mission when former leaders Alison Withers and Matt Smith stepped down after many years of faithful service.

Planning the mission had its challenges. Toby says, 'Covid constraints were constantly changing. In the end, we decided the safest thing was to make our plans using the existing restrictions, in the hope that restrictions would have loosened by the time of the mission itself.

'The biggest issue was having a team half the usual size because we needed to keep them socially distanced and in bubbles. That meant we could only accommodate around 12 people instead of the usual 30. Also, half of that much reduced team was new. Thankfully, the other half really knew the ropes, for which we were so grateful to God!'

Making connections; building relationships

The centrepiece of Polzeath Family Mission used to be the Road Show, a broadcast of the gospel from a stage. However, this would have risked drawing a crowd, which the team considered to be unwise at that point of the pandemic. They would have to adapt and try something new. Fortunately, Toby is no stranger to innovation.

'We set up sports and activities in small groups spread out across the beach: volleyball, football, tennis, building sand marble runs and so on. Most afternoons over a hundred children, young people and families took part. This worked really well, actually, as we wanted to focus on children and young people without a church connection. Having a variety of activities meant our team were able to chat with individual children and bring faith into the conversation more naturally.

'One really interesting aspect of Polzeath is that almost all those who visit the mission are visitors rather than locals. But they're not one-off visitors. Most of the children and young people come with their families to Polzeath for the same week or fortnight every year, staying at the same guest house or in the same caravan. So the great thing is that this summer, we'll be able to build on the relationships we developed with the same children and young people who came last year.'

So open to exploring faith

Each day started with Bible-based sessions for three different age groups. Toby says, 'Initially, most of the children and young people coming to those sessions were from Christian families. Then, as we got to know other children we met at the beach activities, we invited them to come along too. And because they had been playing volleyball or doing other activities alongside the kids from Christian families, it was quite comfortable for them to take that step. So the numbers grew during the week – by the end we had up to 15 children or young people in each group.

'Many of these children without church connections were so open to exploring faith. In one group, we discussed the day of Pentecost in one of the sessions and offered to pray for children individually. The new youngsters wanted prayer too – actually, they had a real hunger for it! On another day, we discussed God's forgiveness. We invited the kids to take a stone from the beach, pray for forgiveness, and then throw the stone far out into the sea as a sign that God would remember their sins no more. The children without church links took part just as enthusiastically as those from Christian families. It's not for me to say that they're now on a journey of faith, but they were clearly very receptive.

'Then there were the two lads that our intern, Matt, met on the beach one afternoon. He was playing football

SU article

with them, and they were chatting together. It turned out that they came from Bristol, and one of them had a connection to one of our other team members. Matt was about to set up a football project in Bristol, so he gave them his details and invited them to contact him when they'd got back home and get involved. And they did! So Matt now has an opportunity to build a relationship with them on their shared home turf, which is great!'

Learning to share faith boldly

Taking part in the Polzeath Family Mission team really benefited Josh, Matt and Ydson, the three SU trainees. Toby says, 'When I asked Josh what he thought the biggest benefit was of being on Polzeath Family Mission team, he said that now he had more self-confidence in stepping out and sharing his faith with complete strangers. He said that on his way home, after the mission, he'd dropped in to see a friend. They had gone for a drink and got talking to a stranger in the pub. It ended up with them praying for him – and Josh's friend says that this man has been going to her church ever since.

'Some weeks later, Josh phoned the family of a young man, who didn't turn up at another of our projects one day, to check if everything was all right. It turned out that the mum was poorly, and so Josh prayed for them over the phone. The mum was so grateful that she was in tears.'

Discovering that God is real

The team were also able to strengthen links with Tubestation, the local beachside church, which doubles as a café and art gallery. A Tubestation volunteer was on the Mission team, and the Bible-based sessions for older teenagers took place in the church garden.

It was there that Tubestation hosted a barbecue one night. Toby recalls, 'They had an impromptu worship session. As I looked around at all the young people, I saw this lad, James, who is in his early teens. We'd met him on the beach and invited him to the Bible sessions, and he'd come along every single day. Now, here he was, absolutely transfixed, with his eyes closed as he drank in the words and music of the worship songs – perhaps discovering for the first time that God is real and present, here and now.

'We can't wait until July and the chance to reconnect with James and the many other children and young people we met last year. We look forward to journeying with them as they explore faith, encounter God and find in him true purpose for their lives.'

A shorter version of this story first appeared in Connecting You, *SU's free quarterly supporter magazine, in winter 2021. If you'd like to receive copies of* Connecting You *and learn more of how God is moving in the hearts and lives of children and young people today, you can sign up online at su.org.uk/ connectingyou.*

'Not with a bang but a whimper'

The title is taken from the final words of the poet TS Eliot's masterpiece, *The Hollow Men* (1925). Eliot's weary conclusion about the world's end could also be used of the main character in this series of readings. King David is nearing the end of his life, and we sense that he is now a broken man. His political and military victories are distant memories. The man who united warring tribes and established a kingdom is now a shadow of his former self.

His daughter Tamar is raped by her half-brother Amnon (2 Samuel 13:1–21), who in turn is then murdered by another one of his sons, Absalom (2 Samuel 13:23–39). Absalom plots a coup d'état against David and comes to a brutal end (2 Samuel 18:9–15). Much of David's history does not make for easy reading, and without giving the game away, this series of readings will feel uncomfortable to our modern western sensibilities.

Themes of revenge and bloodshed abound (chapters 20 and 21), sitting uneasily alongside wonderful songs of praise (chapters 22; 23:1–7). The series ends on an ambivalent note, as David courts the Lord's displeasure by carrying out a national census (chapter 24:10). But despite his many failures, Israel remembered him as their greatest king, and Jesus himself was hailed as a Son of David (eg Matthew 15:22).

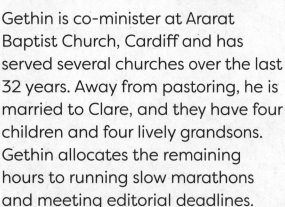

About the writer
Gethin Russell-Jones

Gethin is co-minister at Ararat Baptist Church, Cardiff and has served several churches over the last 32 years. Away from pastoring, he is married to Clare, and they have four children and four lively grandsons. Gethin allocates the remaining hours to running slow marathons and meeting editorial deadlines.

Streetwise God

PREPARE

How real am I before God? With others, we may present ourselves in a certain way and our relationships may seem guarded. Not so with our Father in heaven. Let's pour our hearts out to him in confession and praise.

....

READ

2 Samuel 22:17–30

EXPLORE

Here, David's life signature tune continues. God is faithful to those who are faithful to him (v 26) – whatever our situation, whoever we are with.

I remember hearing once of a pastor, who in her spiritual care of others was exemplary, known to be sincere in her faith and gracious in her relationships. She was also chair of trustees of a significant charity. In this context too, her values and conduct were gracious. She remained open-hearted but was able to manage the charity in an efficient and business-like manner. In other words, she was authentic. Is such faithful consistency evident in our own lives too (vs 21–25)?

Remember the young David, in whom God saw a man after his own heart (1 Samuel 16:7; Acts 13:22)? According to verses 25 and 26, when we live our lives before him as faithful, authentic and pure-hearted people (v 27), then he, in turn, meets us in the same spirit. But notice, where there is hypocrisy or guile, he is not taken in and we will find it hard to connect with him (vs 27,28).

'To the faithful you show yourself faithful, to the blameless you show yourself blameless.'

2 Samuel 22:26

RESPOND

'Lord, in the simplicity of this moment, I set aside all pretence and hypocrisy as I pour out my heart to you – my strengths and my weaknesses.'

....

Bible in a year: Isaiah 61,62; Hebrews 12

Sunday 2 October
Psalm 65

Praise is rising

PREPARE
Wherever I am, I still myself and listen to my breathing. As I breathe in and out, I give thanks to God for this gift of life. I praise him that he sustains and provides for all that he has made.

. . . .

READ
Psalm 65

EXPLORE
I have a penchant for crime drama, particularly the stories where the initial incident escalates into the world of politics and the media. This was the approach taken, for example, by the hugely successful Danish TV series *The Killing,* and by *Spiral*, a French production. This psalm uses the same dynamic but for good purposes.

We start in the Temple in Jerusalem, where the psalmist rejoices that God answers prayer and forgives all who call on him, and he is happy simply to be in this sacred space (vs 1–4). But the bulk of the poem takes us way beyond the Temple mount. We are spiralled into the whole of creation to see God's loving exercised in favour of all that he has made.

Mountains, seas, animals, the planet and its peoples are all the beneficiaries of this lavish providence. And this grace provokes a response from beyond the Temple walls. We are told that songs of joy come from the whole earth and that even the fields, meadows and valleys shout for joy. Wherever I find myself on this earth, praise is always rising.

The whole earth is filled with awe at your wonders; where morning dawns, where evening fades, you call forth songs of joy.

Psalm 65:8

RESPOND
'Show me how I – along with all your people and with all of creation – can praise you with my whole life.'

. . . .

Bible in a year: Isaiah 63,64; Hebrews 13

Standing strong

PREPARE

Lord, you are my rock and my strong tower. You see what I cannot, and you work on a canvas that is vast and infinite. God of love and mercy, I choose to submit to your will and purposes today.

. . . .

READ

2 Samuel 22:31–51

EXPLORE

This long psalm – also included in the book of Psalms (Psalm 18) – gives an epic and poetic account of God's dealings with David in praise for his rescue from his enemies. As he looks back over turbulent times, the poet is able to see God's hand in his life in the most trying and desperate of circumstances. And we remind ourselves that this song of thanksgiving came out of a long period of being hunted down by his former mentor, King Saul.

In praising God for keeping him steady and strong when he might have collapsed, he employs a metaphor that is used elsewhere in the Old Testament. He says that God makes his feet like a deer's, able to scale high places (v 34). This word picture can also be found in Habakkuk 3:19.

In her bestselling book *Hinds Feet on High Places* (Christian Literature Crusade, 1955), Hannah Hurnard tells the story of Much Afraid and her many ordeals. In the company of two friends – Sorrow and Suffering – she discovers that God is indeed able to give her grip and strength on the dazzling heights of her life.

'For who is God besides the LORD? And who is the Rock except our God?'

2 Samuel 22:32

RESPOND

'Lord, I am uncertain and tentative about many things. But I look to you as my helper and guide to give me the courage I need today.'

. . . .

Bible in a year: Isaiah 65,66; John 1

Tuesday 4 October

2 Samuel 23:1–7

A sober assessment

PREPARE

Lord, the giver of life, I thank you for my life. I remember that this is your gift to me and that the lives of those whom I love and who love me are also part of your storehouse of gifts.

....

READ

2 Samuel 23:1–7

EXPLORE

This section is introduced as David's last words, but there's no indication in this short poem that he is on his death bed (see also 1 Kings 2:1–12). It may be that he composed it earlier in his career, and it was placed towards the end of his life.

As with all of David's psalms, it's a thing of literary and spiritual beauty. The imagery used and the sense of confidence in God bear all the hallmarks of David's powerful, creative gifts. And he begins with a sober assessment of himself. He is an ordinary son of an ordinary father but elevated to a great honour by the God of his ancestors. His anointing as king is the work of God and not of his doing (vs 1–3,5).

More than anything else, it seems, he wants to be remembered as a singer. One version of verse 1 says 'I am Israel's most popular singer' (*The Message*). Not a statesman, military ruler or king, but a singer of songs. I wonder how we might describe ourselves to others?

These are the last words of David: 'The inspired utterance of David son of Jesse, the utterance of the man exalted by the Most High...'

2 Samuel 23:1a

RESPOND

God looks at your heart and sees your impulses towards worship, prayer and intimacy with him. He sees your relationships with others. What do these things say about you and the way you handle life?

....

Bible in a year: Jeremiah 1,2; Psalms 112,113

Very gallant gentlemen

PREPARE

'I still my heart, Lord, and ask now that you would make me aware of your presence. You are always with me, but there are many times in the day when I feel far away from you. I turn to you now.'

READ

2 Samuel 23:8–23

EXPLORE

On 15 June 1910, the SS *Terra Nova* left Cardiff docks as the crew embarked on their ill-fated expedition to Antarctica. Under the leadership of Captain Robert Falcon Scott (1868–1912), they hoped to be the first to set foot at the South Pole, but it turned out to be a doomed endeavour.

In a lake in one of Cardiff's loveliest public parks, there stands a lighthouse commemorating this voyage. In an inscription remembering the small crew, it concludes by saying, 'Britons all, and very gallant gentlemen.' None returned and all perished, and so, every time I visit this place, I am grateful that they have been named and are remembered.

Today's reading serves a similar function. These are David's friends and colleagues who risked their lives for him, and we remember them, thousands of years later. There are many such lists in the Bible: genealogies, accounts of military success or names that mark the slow trudge of history. It's a reminder that no one is nameless or faceless before God.

These are the last words of David: '… the man anointed by the God of Jacob, the hero of Israel's songs.'

2 Samuel 23:1b

RESPOND

If you were to draw up a list of the most significant people to have influenced you across your life, who would they be? Name them before God and give thanks for them.

Bible in a year: Jeremiah 3,4; John 2

Thursday 6 October
2 Samuel 24:1–17

Me and my shadow

PREPARE

'I don't want to cloak my sins as I come before you, Lord. I have wandered from your ways, and there is no health in me. Have mercy on me, according to your great loving kindness shown in Jesus. Amen.'

....

READ

2 Samuel 24:1–17

EXPLORE

This is an example of another story that occurs earlier in David's life, reported beginning at 1 Chronicles 21:1. The implementation of a military census to recruit more soldiers probably doesn't strike us as a sign of spiritual compromise, but this is exactly how God views it. Why so?

Joab, David's commander-in-chief, seems to get to the heart of it (v 3). If you need more fighting men, God will give them to you, but this seems like you're going behind his back. In other words, David isn't trusting God with his needs. This has been a theme in David's life, manipulating events for his own gain. His affair with Bathsheba and its aftermath is another example of this (2 Samuel 11).

Psychologists often refer to the 'shadow' side of our personalities: habits, motives and actions that we try to conceal but which often influence our lives, sometimes unconsciously. David is confronted about the shadow side of his personality and learns the hard way. Have there been times in your life when you too have seen the poverty of your motives and desires?

...'I have sinned greatly in what I have done. Now, LORD, I beg you, take away the guilt of your servant. I have done a very foolish thing.'

2 Samuel 24:10

RESPOND

'With you is grace, Lord, wide and free. I gladly confess to you that I am in need of your Holy Spirit to make me whole.'

....

Bible in a year: Jeremiah 5,6; John 3

Costly worship

PREPARE
'Fear not to enter his courts in the slenderness of the poor wealth thou wouldst reckon as thine: truth in its beauty and love in its tenderness, these are the offerings to lay on his shrine.'*

. . . .

READ
2 Samuel 24:18–24

EXPLORE
This effectively marks the final major incident in David's life. Given a choice between three punishments for grieving God in the matter of the census, he opts for the shortest. And probably the deadliest: a three-day pandemic that will sweep through the country. But when David sees the angel of the Lord poised to destroy Jerusalem, he pleads for mercy and is allowed to make a burnt offering to the Lord.

All this takes place on the threshing floor of Araunah the Jebusite. This was on Mount Moriah, the hill to the east of Jerusalem, and was the site upon which the Temple was built afterwards (2 Chronicles 3:1). Jewish tradition identified this with the mountain which was the scene of the sacrifice of Isaac (Genesis 22:2).

Some places carry memories of worship and encounter with the living God. David's last act is his remembrance of meeting the grace of God in the midst of his failure. This is where the Temple will be built but not by him.

But the king replied to Araunah, 'No, I insist on paying you for it. I will not sacrifice to the LORD my God burnt offerings that cost me nothing.'

2 Samuel 24:24

RESPOND
Have there been places where you have met God and the course of your life has changed direction? Call them to mind, remember the story, and thank God for his involvement in your life.

*'O Worship the Lord in the Beauty of Holiness', John SB Monsell (1811–1875).

. . . .

Bible in a year: Jeremiah 7,8; Psalms 114,115

My dear son

A couple of the books I've enjoyed have been written as correspondence: the real-life *84 Charing Cross Road* (Helene Hanff), published in 1970 but written from 1949 onwards, and the more recent, fictional, *Meet Me at the Museum* (Anne Youngson, 2018). In both, friendship slowly grows between two strangers, and satisfying relationships ensue.

About the writer
Gill Robertson

Gill is a 60-something, recently retired vicar's wife, step-mother and fairly new grandmother; and a Lay Reader (LLM). She is also a musician, composer, crafter and cook; and the time spent on these activities is inversely proportional to that spent on housework!

Paul's letters to Timothy are two of the four epistles written as letters to individuals (the other two being Titus and Philemon). They are written, however, as a result of the existing relationship between the two, developed through Paul's second and third missionary journeys. Rick Warren likens their relationship to mentoring and suggests it began as 'parenting' – a young disciple with an older one, grown through 'pace-setting' – Paul setting Timothy an example to follow, resulting in 'partnering' – with them being co-workers (https://pastors.com/paul-timothy/). While this second letter is written in that last stage, close to the end of Paul's life, his ongoing deep affection for Timothy as a son in faith is evident, as is his deep desire for Timothy to stand firm, even through suffering, and to teach the truth and fulfil his calling. The first letter contained advice regarding leadership and church matters. This one is more personal, more concerned with Timothy's own faith and the challenges leadership brings.

Whether young or older as a person, or as a disciple of Christ, and whatever position we may have in church, I pray we will all benefit as we consider Paul's wisdom to his younger, much-loved friend.

Flames of faith

PREPARE
Remember those who have had an impact on your growth in faith. Was it something they said, or did, or their example in another way? Was it over a period of time or a single event? Give thanks for them.

READ
2 Timothy 1:1–7

EXPLORE
For some reason, the fire of Timothy's faith seems, perhaps, to be just gently smouldering when Paul was writing this second letter to him. It had first been sparked into life by his mother and grandmother (v 5). The first verses of today's reading are a touching tribute to the spiritual influence they had had on his early life. Paul himself addresses Timothy as his 'dear son' – a term of affection that indicates the depth of relationship they'd developed.

Because of that, Paul can remind Timothy that things should burn more brightly again – specifically, the gift given to him by God (v 6). This is unspecified, but we can speculate that it's connected with his role in the church as a leader – for which the attributes in verse 7 are important and need wielding carefully. If Timothy has been called to the responsibility of leading and has been given a spiritual gift by God – which he has – then that gift needs to be fanned back into bright flame. Then he can fulfil what God has called him to with enthusiasm and energy (v 14).

> For this reason I remind you to fan into flame the gift of God, which is in you through the laying on of my hands.
>
> **2 Timothy 1:6**

RESPOND
Think about who God has called you to be and what he has called you to do. Is that burning down, or flaming up? Ask God to bless you with encouragement from others, whatever state your 'fire' is in.

Bible in a year: Jeremiah 9,10; John 4

Sunday 9 October
Psalm 66

Song of praise

PREPARE

'Shout to the Lord, all the earth, let us sing power and majesty, praise to the King.'* Use this song, or another that praises God joyfully, to acknowledge his greatness and come into his presence in worship.

•••

READ
Psalm 66

EXPLORE

This psalm burns brightly with joy in the Lord and aims to inspire the glorious praise of his name. It invites people to discover for themselves who God is and what God has done (vs 5,16). It gives details of his powerful acts for his people (vs 6,9,19,20). It acknowledges the testing and generosity of the Lord (vs 10–12) and promises offerings to the one who listens and answers (vs 13–15,19). It brings a wonderful sense of the writer and his confidence in proclaiming God. It is full of worship to the Lord for all he has done.

Paul knew the psalms. You can imagine that this one might be exactly the sort of psalm that he would direct Timothy to, to help rekindle the fire of his faith. All of us have times when passion for God and his kingdom may burn lower than at others. As you reflect on this psalm, let it remind you of the Lord and 'his awesome deeds for mankind' (v 5) – and for you.

Come and see what God has done, his awesome deeds for mankind!

Psalm 66:5

RESPOND

Spend some time writing your own psalm and thanks to God. Whether your faith could be described as embers or a blazing fire right now, let it remind you of who the Lord is and why you're his follower.

*'My Jesus, My Saviour', Darlene Zschech, © 1993, Wondrous Worship.

•••

Bible in a year: Jeremiah 11,12; John 5

'I have confidence in...'

PREPARE
On her way to the Trapp family, Maria (Julie Andrews, *The Sound of Music*) sang that she had confidence in herself – boosting herself against nervousness by singing, 'I can *do* this!' What things about yourself do you have confidence in? Why?

READ
2 Timothy 1:8–18

EXPLORE
Paul's great confidence in the gospel shines through these words. He can even welcome his suffering because of the reason it is happening (v 8). His whole focus here is good news in Jesus, encapsulated in verse 10. That leads him to have this confidence in who he is, not who he is in his own strength, or in his own abilities, but because of who he is *in Christ* (v 11). He knows that what strengths he has are because of Jesus.

Paul wrote in Romans 12 that we should not think of ourselves more highly than we ought (Romans 12:3). His words here also imply that we should have a *right* opinion of ourselves, one which recognises who and what we are in Christ – we are the result 'of his own purpose and grace' (v 9). Paul is confident in his salvation, his calling and appointing; confident in his message and is confident that his suffering –

abandoned (v 15) and in prison – is part of that. Notice, too, Paul's thankfulness to Onesiphorus – 'not ashamed' – whose humble faithfulness has helped him in this work of the gospel (vs 16–18).

> I know whom I have believed, and am convinced that he is able to guard what I have entrusted to him until that day.
>
> **2 Timothy 1:12**

RESPOND
What are your abilities, strengths and weaknesses? In prayer, offer these again to him, asking God to use them as he chooses, for the sake of the gospel.

Bible in a year: Jeremiah 13,14; John 6

2 Timothy 2:1–13

Fight, train, dig

PREPARE
How would you complete these sentences? 'A Christian is like…', 'Being a Christian is like…', 'The life of faith is like…' Which pictures or other analogies might you use to describe these things?

....

READ
2 Timothy 2:1–13

EXPLORE
Paul uses three striking and contrasting types of people to help us understand what it means to be a believer: a soldier, who must be fit, obey orders and, at some point, fight; an athlete, who must train and compete according to the rules; and a farmer, who must till the land and sow in season to reap a crop. Each then receives their reward: the approval of the commanding officer, receiving a victor's crown and having the first share of the harvest.

Each image also involves hard work and hardship. None of those successes – approval, victory and a share in the harvest – are easily attained. Paul is clear with Timothy that there's a need for strength and endurance if the gospel is to be proclaimed, and people are to find salvation in Christ Jesus. For anyone who wants a faith that demands little of them, these words are challenging.

Suffering because of the hard work of faith is pretty much inevitable, but the rewards are out of this world (vs 10–12)!

Therefore I endure everything for the sake of the elect, that they too may obtain the salvation that is in Christ Jesus, with eternal glory.

2 Timothy 2:10

RESPOND
Which of the three images would you most align yourself with? A fighter, someone who trains, or a digger? Pray that God would help you to accept and grow in and through the challenges that following Jesus brings.

....

Bible in a year: Jeremiah 15,16; Psalm 116

Hold fast

PREPARE
Have you ever had to defend yourself against someone's false accusation? Or listened to someone speaking confidently – but in complete error – about something? How should we respond in this situation?

· ·

READ
2 Timothy 2:14–19

EXPLORE
At the heart of this passage there is another striking image – an unpleasant, corruptive, decaying image: gangrene (v 17). An internet search will show how gangrene affects the body. Be warned, there are some really horrible pictures.

This awful image gives us an insight into how very serious Paul considered 'godless chatter' (v 16) and false teaching to be (vs 17,18) and how important it was, therefore, to encourage Timothy to 'correctly handle the word of truth' (v 15). Like gangrene, false teaching eventually kills off faith, and Paul wanted the body of Christ to be healthy. More specifically, the teaching by the two named individuals that the resurrection – here referring to the future bodily resurrection of all believers – had already happened had destroyed some people's faith (vs 17,18). Timothy's responsibility was to keep declaring what he knows is the truth; to keep standing on the solid foundation of the church (1 Timothy 3:15), in the knowledge of God's protection as he does so.

> Do your best to present yourself to God as one approved, a worker who does not need to be ashamed and who correctly handles the word of truth.
>
> **2 Timothy 2:15**

RESPOND
Today, there are contentious issues under discussion in the church; issues that can and do cause division and distress. Pray today that those participating would seek to 'correctly handle the word of truth'.

· ·

Bible in a year: Jeremiah 17,18; John 7

Thursday 13 October

2 Timothy 2:20–26

Held to high standards

PREPARE

Who was your favourite teacher at school? What qualities made them stand out? Who helps you now to learn and grow in your faith as a Christian?

....

READ

2 Timothy 2:20–26

EXPLORE

If you've had a good teacher, you'll know that they encourage you to want to learn; to do better; to get things right. Learning – in my experience at least – is never achieved by being cross with students for not understanding, or for taking too long, for finding it hard or for… anything else. Maybe that's true for the Christian life too.

Paul reminds Timothy that kindness and gentleness are better ways to accomplish someone's discovery of their need to repent and believe in the truth (vs 24,25). These are also better ways of confronting opposition to the gospel. To prepare for being that kind of teacher, Paul advises him that endless arguments or quarrels about pointless and trivial matters achieve nothing (v 23). His initial instructions to be cleansed from those things which defile and to seek for spiritual fruit among the company of those who do the same (vs 21,22) will set

Timothy on the right path as a teacher of the truth. While Paul is writing to him as a church leader, we're all teachers of faith in some ways, so this applies to each of us.

And the Lord's servant must not be quarrelsome but must be kind to everyone, able to teach, not resentful.

2 Timothy 2:24

RESPOND

Sadly, there are Christian leaders whose private lives do not match their public personas. Pray for all who teach God's Word to be willing to cleanse themselves first, so they may be as verse 21 describes.

....

Bible in a year: Jeremiah 19,20; John 8

Same old, same old...

PREPARE
How do you react to someone who tries to manipulate you, treats you unkindly, or whose way of life is utterly focused on themselves?

....

READ
2 Timothy 3:1–9

EXPLORE
In the fourth century BC, Plato had a go at the youth of the day. In AD 1274, so did Peter the Hermit. Their remarks have sometimes been quoted anonymously, as if written about people nowadays, with the reveal of their origins coming later. And oh, what a surprise! People (and not just young people) have been acting the same way from time immemorial to the present day.

Paul's list of activities and attitudes to be avoided is awful, whichever translation of the Bible you read it from. (*The Message* paraphrase is particularly graphic!) The kinds of behaviours described are, of course, damaging to the people who behave like that and damaging to those on the receiving end, who are prevented from finding the truth (v 7). No wonder Paul advises Timothy to steer clear – run away (vs 5; 2:22)! What's worse is that in 'having a form of godliness but denying its power' (v 5), such people are engaged in the rituals of worship but refuse to let God change them into who he created them to be – denying his power to redeem and renew.

> ... having a form of godliness but denying its power.

2 Timothy 3:5

RESPOND
Honestly? Some of these behaviours might be ours, on occasion. But when we recognise it and seek forgiveness, the saving grace and mercy of God comes to meet us and transform us into the likeness of Christ. Ask God for his forgiveness now.

....

Bible in a year: Jeremiah 21,22; Psalms 117,118

Saturday 15 October
2 Timothy 3:10–17

Book learning

PREPARE
What's your favourite book from childhood? Your favourite book as an adult? Your favourite book of the Bible? (Mine is Nehemiah.) Why?

....

READ
2 Timothy 3:10–17

EXPLORE
Paul is clear that the kinds of people we read about yesterday aren't going anywhere (v 13). And the effects of those people on the lives of those who follow Jesus are, sadly, inevitable. Persecution is to be expected (v 12). Paul therefore urges Timothy to keep focused on scripture – on what he has learned from being an infant (vs 14,15), so that verse 17 is the result.

Two things occur to me. One is that it's *all* scripture – not just the bits we like, but the bits that challenge or make us feel uncomfortable too. Of course, we need to approach the more difficult passages carefully and, if necessary, with help, but avoiding them isn't helpful.

The second is to think about what 'every good work' might actually be (v 17). We might really, really like what he calls us to, or the place he wants us in, or the people he puts us with. But sometimes we might not. Good works for God sometimes take us right out of our comfort zone, and scripture, in all its fullness and variety, helps us to be ready.

> ... so that the servant of God may be thoroughly equipped for every good work.
>
> **2 Timothy 3:17**

RESPOND
Pray today for Christians whom God has called to work in challenging circumstances: perhaps physically or in places where God's Word and God's people are viewed with suspicion or hostility.

....

Bible in a year: Jeremiah 23,24; John 9

Bless you!

PREPARE

'Bless the Lord, Oh my soul, oh my soul, worship his holy name.'* Think about the reasons you have to bless the Lord, and sing them with fervour as you come into God's presence.

....

READ
Psalm 67

EXPLORE

This psalm, to be accompanied with guitars, violins and any other stringed instrument you can name, is a lovely poem asking God to bless his people. The first verse is a reminder of the blessing in Numbers 6:24–26 – the priestly blessing – and the psalmist clearly longs for everyone, everywhere, to praise the Lord. Two reasons are given: the justice and guidance of God (v 4), and the blessing of harvest (v 6), which we're celebrating again around this time of year. There's also a sense that the blessing of God on his people, when it comes, is to be a witness to the world, a testimony to the love of God for his people (vs 2,7).

Paul wrote to Timothy twice, and both letters open with Paul asking for the blessing of 'Grace, mercy and peace from God the Father and Christ Jesus our Lord' (2 Timothy 1:2) to be upon his dear son in the faith. That's something we might well consider beginning with next time we're in touch with someone!

> May God be gracious to us and bless us and make his face shine on us.
>
> **Psalm 67:1**

RESPOND

With the immediacy of multiple types of communication available to us today, we may sometimes plunge straight in without any opening 'Hello, how are you?' preamble. Take time to write a card or letter today, just asking God to bless someone.

*'10,000 Reasons', Jonas Myrin and Matt Redman, © 2011, Thankyou Music.

....

Bible in a year: Jeremiah 25,26; John 10

Monday 17 October

2 Timothy 4:1–8

Stay on track

PREPARE

How focused are you on completing God's work and preparing others to be ready for its challenge?

READ

2 Timothy 4:1–8

EXPLORE

There's both confidence and poignancy in the way Paul speaks to Timothy in verses 6–8. Tom Wright comments that 'Paul lived his life with the clock ticking in the background'* – and it's clear that he thinks his life on earth will come to an end before long. He uses two of his previous analogies – those of soldier and athlete (v 7) – to describe how fully he has followed Jesus since he met him on the road to Damascus (Acts 9:1–19). He is confident that the Lord will reward him for his faithful service (v 8).

Because of this and because judgement is coming (v 1), he charges Timothy with the words in verse 2 (and you could write several sermons just on that one verse!). He wants to be sure that Timothy will continue with the work Paul has trained and mentored him for. It's almost a passing on of the mantle, such as with Elijah to Elisha (2 Kings 2:1–18). Timothy needs to be ready for the challenge of those who only want to hear doctrine that suits them and to stay focused on the work he is called to (v 5).

> I have fought the good fight, I have finished the race, I have kept the faith.
>
> **2 Timothy 4:7**

RESPOND

Pray verse 5 for yourself, substituting whatever God has called you to, if not 'evangelist'. Pray, too, that the good news of Jesus will characterise and shine through all 'the duties of your ministry'.

*Tom Wright, *Paul for Everyone: The Pastoral Letters* (2003), SPCK Publishing.

Bible in a year: Jeremiah 27,28; John 11

And finally...

PREPARE
Do you write a round-robin letter at Christmas? If yes, what kind of details do you include? What might key differences be if you were writing just to your Christian family?

READ
2 Timothy 4:9–22

EXPLORE
This final passage in 2 Timothy brims with small, endearing and personal matters. They give us a glimpse of Paul the man, rather than Paul the apostle. There are details of things he's missing (v 13). There is commendation and condemnation (vs 11,14,15). There are greetings to and from friends (vs 19–21). And there's a sense of loneliness and longing for his 'dear son' (vs 9,11,21).

All of this paints a picture of the joy and the cost of ministry. The middle verses (vs 16–18) describe how he felt abandoned by everyone who could have supported him at his first defence and look with certain hope to the promise of heaven. Central to that is the Lord, right beside him (v 17), strengthening and enabling him to overcome and complete his ministry.

The sign-off to this second letter to Timothy reveals the heart of Paul: his love and encouragement of those who work alongside him for the sake of the gospel, and his utter confidence in the Lord he trusts.

> But the Lord stood at my side and gave me strength, so that through me the message might be fully proclaimed...
>
> **2 Timothy 4:17**

RESPOND
Pray today for your church leaders and those you work alongside. Ask God to strengthen them in their ministry and to give them encouragement and blessing. Ask God how you can be a part of doing that.

Bible in a year: Jeremiah 29–31; Psalm 119:1–24

Scripture Union

A legacy of love

Could you leave a gift in your will and ensure the good news of Jesus is shared with generations to come?

TO FIND OUT MORE, VISIT SU.ORG.UK/LEGACY OR CALL 01908 856120

'...we will tell the next generation the praiseworthy deeds of the Lord, his power, and the wonders he has done.' **Psalm 78:4**

A man faithful to the end

About the writer
Mike Hawthorne

After many years of mission in Asia, Mike and his wife, Sue, have settled into a large, rambly old house in Herefordshire, which they use for various types of hospitality ministry.

We love it when we sense that the Scriptures are speaking personally to us – and quite right too. God is indeed alive and still at work through his Word and through ordinary people. Jeremiah is a vulnerable character, quite shy and, at times, uncertain. These are not factors which matter to God, who calls Jeremiah to an inspired, dynamic ministry. Wonderful – these are all aspects we shall explore in the coming days, and we shall find that the book of Jeremiah is bang up to date.

That said, it is also important to acknowledge that these words are coming to us from the deep mists of time. As Jeremiah lamented the downfall of Israel, Ancient Britons were plodding through the Iron Age. Modern assumptions may well be unhelpful. I just referred to a 'book' but, in truth, no such thing existed in Old Testament times. We should not always expect clear narrative sequence or a logical development of ideas in Jeremiah. Nor should we be shocked if the people in these passages behave and express feelings in ways which seem alien or even disgusting to us. Let me declare, as we start, that there are things here which I do not understand. However, there is also much, on every page, through which the Holy Spirit can minister to his church. So let us approach this sacred text with awe and humility but also with confidence. People have not changed so very much since Jeremiah's day – and our wise and loving God not one bit.

Wednesday 19 October
Jeremiah 18:1–12; 19:1–13

Clay in God's hands

PREPARE
Without detailed thought, how would you answer the question: 'What sort of personality does God have?' Take a minute to reflect on your answer before reading today's verses.

. . . .

READ
Jeremiah 18:1–12; 19:1–13

EXPLORE
There is a huge and fascinating issue for anyone studying the Bible as a whole, and it is one which Christians sometimes avoid. On the one hand, we hold firmly to our idea of a God who is gracious and loving. On the other (unless we are very determined cherry pickers), we must face the reality that so much Old Testament material describes a God who seems violent and angry. For starters today, we read the prophecy that God will make his people become cannibals, eating their own children (19:9). How can this be?

Today's passage affirms first, the truth that God is absolute sovereign (18:5–10). It is for him to decide how to order the universe he created and not for us to challenge him. Indeed, we are, in more ways than one, 'like clay in the hand' (18:6). These verses demonstrate equally the deep wickedness of humankind.

Read carefully and it becomes clear that each one of the horrors here is a consequence of human behaviour (19:4,5). *Of course*, our loving God wills nothing but good for his people. Then the deal – set forth at our creation – is that we can choose good or evil. The miracle of the gospel is that God himself stands ready (18:8) to change his plans for us.

'Can I not do with you, Israel, as this potter does?' declares the Lord. 'Like clay in the hand of the potter, so are you in my hand, Israel.'
Jeremiah 18:6

> ## RESPOND
> Pray that God spares our own nation the deserved fate of ancient Israel.

. . . .

Bible in a year: Jeremiah 32,33; John 12

Be yourself

PREPARE
Give your grimmest, saddest thoughts to the Lord, and ask him to look after them.

READ
Jeremiah 20:1–18

EXPLORE
OK, so today we have a thoroughly nasty priest, close relatives accursed, suicidal thoughts from our battered hero and, worst of all, God apparently as deceiver (v 7). How dare Jeremiah say these things? And how do the lovely, sporadic verses 11 and 13 fit in between so much disgrace, wailing and vengeance? But this is the Bible. All reality is here – and the ancient writers are under no obligation to conform to our polite literary conventions. Perhaps if we could ask him about this passage, Jeremiah would reply, 'I know God well enough, and he knows how I felt on that terrible day. Should I not have declared my heart?' (v 9).

The truth is that dark things come into the heads of most modern, educated people, which we dare not admit that we think – perhaps fully even to ourselves. Christians are not exempt. The inclination of many is to push such ideas straight back down and to dwell, rather, upon the 'excellent and praiseworthy' (Philippians 4:8). This is a biblical principle greatly to be recommended. However, it is not enough simply to ignore the dark side. The Bible never does so. Rather, Jeremiah chooses a spiritual path, which takes him *through* his own and his nation's anguish, always looking ahead to God's deliverance and glory (v 13).

> But the LORD is with me like a mighty warrior; so my persecutors ... will fail and be thoroughly disgraced; their dishonour will never be forgotten.
>
> **Jeremiah 20:11**

RESPOND
Contemplate, for some time, the truth that God's complete and final victory will come.

Bible in a year: Jeremiah 34,35; John 13

Friday 21 October
Jeremiah 21:1–14

No justice: no future

PREPARE
How do you understand the idea of justice? Does it apply differently to individuals and to nations?

....

READ
Jeremiah 21:1–14

EXPLORE
This is the very end of the history of Judah as a nation. (Remember that Jeremiah's book is not chronological.) The prophet might well have seen the irony, as now, finding themselves in desperate straits, the leading officials finally come to him for advice (vs 1,2). There is also a melancholy about the wistful thought of the king: 'Perhaps God will do wonders as he has in the past.' Whatever they deserve, it is sad to contemplate the fate of Judah.

The people's shared memory, steeped in the stories and glories of Gideon, Joshua and David, is now diminished as they face ignominious defeat. Will God still be absent? It's worse – God is there but on the enemy's side (vs 3–10)! His righteous plan is for his people's exile. Losing their land, independence and freedom will actually be better for the people in the long run. This is what Zedekiah is unwilling to hear. How often do we reject God's guidance because it is not what we hope for and because we cannot yet comprehend the bigger picture?

Overlaying this story of national defeat and humiliation is another idea. Leaving aside current affairs, verse 12 declares an eternal principle, one we can strive for regardless of our circumstances. 'Administer justice every morning,' say the Scriptures, again and again (v 12).

> 'Administer justice every morning; rescue from the hand of the oppressor the one who has been robbed...'
> **Jeremiah 21:12**

RESPOND
Reflect, too, on Micah 6:8, Amos 5:24 and Luke 18:1–8. What are the implications of these words for our lives today?

....

Bible in a year: Jeremiah 36,37; Psalm 119:25–48

God's holy nation

PREPARE
What are the factors that inhibit justice in modern nation states?

. . . .

READ
Jeremiah 22:1–30

EXPLORE
Since the beginnings of our history, humankind has organised itself into nations. Israel was special in the ancient world because (albeit rather on and off) it acknowledged the headship of the one true God. In many other ways, it was just one people among many. It is worth exploring whether we can find out God's ideas about how a proper nation should function: what is the point of these 'nation' entities?

Apparently, at the very heart of the purpose of a nation is the establishment and pursuit of justice. It was originally against the Lord's advice that the Israelites chose to have a king (1 Samuel 8), but sometimes he is gracious enough to go along with our wishes and make the best of our less-than-ideal arrangements. Here, God seems willing to allow the rich and privileged to swagger in and out of the gates (v 2), presumably in the ancient equivalent of a Rolls-Royce, and to live in some sort of pre-Christian Beverley Hills (v 14) so long as they take responsibility for administering justice, in particular to the powerless and the poor (v 3). According to Jeremiah, to be a true king is synonymous with knowing God: such a ruler will care first about justice and caring for the poor. Modern national leaders might want to take note of what happens to those who override this divine principle (vs 13–30).

O land, land, land, hear the word of the LORD!
Jeremiah 22:29

> ## RESPOND
> Pray for justice, especially for those listed in verse 3, who are no less numerous today.

. . . .

Bible in a year: Jeremiah 38,39; John 14

Sunday 23 October
Psalm 68

God in action

PREPARE
If you had to choose music to accompany a Christian march, what would it be?

....

READ
Psalm 68

EXPLORE
Sometimes it's right to face head-on the puzzles and challenges in the Scriptures. Other days, it is fine to simply accept the blessing of discovering more about God and his goodness. Psalm 68 is rich in eternal truths. The psalm begins with a call for God to arise, to manifest himself (vs 1–3). In so many ways, the following verses can be seen as an answer to that prayer. See whether you can locate the following in today's psalm.

First, God's enemies are blown away and melted. It is not even a contest. Then, to his own people, he is the ultimate source of joy and singing. (It is thought that this psalm might have been sung as the Ark of the Covenant was carried up to Jerusalem, 2 Samuel 6:12.) Next, we find a wonderful account of the Lord we can know for real but whom no one would imagine. In one verse he is the classic divine being 'who rides on the clouds' (v 4) but then, in the next breath, he is the one who cares for orphans, captives and the lonely. He makes the earth shake but then waters it, giving special attention to the land of the poor. He steps down from leading his millions of chariots in order to personally carry our burdens. Awesome beyond our conceiving – yet he delights to save the smallest among us.

> Sing to God, sing in praise of his name, extol him who rides on the clouds; rejoice before him – his name is the LORD.
>
> **Psalm 68:4**

RESPOND
As you praise the Lord, picture the procession detailed in verses 24–27.

....

Bible in a year: Jeremiah 40,41; John 15

Shepherds and kings

PREPARE
Would you prefer to live with shepherds or in the court of a king?

READ
Jeremiah 23:1–8

EXPLORE

These verses focus on two ideas that are developed throughout the Scriptures: kingship and shepherding. Moses was a shepherd before he led Israel. David held both positions – and then, of course, shepherds were summoned to the crib to see the King of kings. These days, we know broadly what the words king and shepherd mean, but we are oddities, perhaps at the end of history. We do not live with monarchs who – for better or worse – command absolute power over our lives. Nor do we locally depend on shepherds as skilled but humble guardians of the flocks we need for survival. Any child in either ancient Israel or medieval England reading this account would say, 'Oh yes. Right.' Our own experience is more likely to be of bureaucracies and supermarkets, but the ancient imagery remains powerful and true.

Here, Jeremiah wants us to grasp the essence of both shepherding and kingship so that we can see something of the nature of God himself. The Lord is the ultimate shepherd. His desire is to gather us, care for us, and see us prosper. He embodies true kingship: he is righteous, wise and just (v 5). Ultimately, this is a prophecy about Jesus himself. The Shepherd King will not only be for the original Israelites, but for all of us.

'I will place shepherds over them who will tend them, and they will no longer be afraid or terrified, nor will any be missing,' declares the Lord.
Jeremiah 23:4

RESPOND
Verse 4 promises shepherds to tend God's sheep. Reflect on the meaning of that special word, *tend*.

Bible in a year: Jeremiah 42,43; John 16

Tuesday 25 October
Jeremiah 23:9–32

False prophets

PREPARE
How should Christians respond to the threats of 'fake news' and the obvious distortion in our modern media?

....

READ
Jeremiah 23:9–32

EXPLORE
Here we seem to have a passage without even a shimmer of optimism. Many of us find the tough chunks of the Old Testament manageable because of the lovely, often unexpected glimpses of hope and blessing. There are few of those for us today. On and on runs Jeremiah in his condemnation of his falsely prophesying colleagues. Lies, adultery, idolatry, stubbornness, boasting; Jeremiah's imagery is graphic. We can only conclude that all this must be important. We need to grasp the shocking reality. The prophets themselves have betrayed their people and their God.

What is a prophet? You could look up some definitions, but often, they are said to be those who speak the very mind of God. Great figures among them bestride the Old Testament (definitely not all bearded; women were included) and then of course there is the gift of prophecy given to Jesus' followers. It is a special type of evil, then, if these chosen servants turn bad. For Jeremiah in particular, it is not hard to understand why his heart is broken (v 9). These are his own people, quite possibly friends with whom he has studied and worshipped. The consequences are appalling too. Notice that these include not only exhibitions of divine wrath (vs 19,20), but also more prosaic, but horrible, effects on the land itself (v 10).

'See, the storm of the LORD will burst out in wrath, a whirlwind swirling down on the heads of the wicked.'
Jeremiah 23:19

RESPOND
Pray for the leaders of the church today, that they may be strengthened and protected and may remain faithful.

....

Bible in a year: Jeremiah 44–46; Psalm 119:49–72

To give a fig

PREPARE
Would you be prepared to move house for God? What if your new home was less comfortable?

. . . .

READ
Jeremiah 24:1–10

EXPLORE
In typical Jeremiah fashion, we have now jumped forward to a point when the rulers and elites of the nation have been carted off into exile (v 1). Perhaps to some despairing Israelites, it felt like the end of their story. Not so, of course. One wonder of the Scriptures is that they provide us with a God's-eye view – and, even for non-believers, surely a marvel of history is that the saga of Israel continues to this day.

No prizes for working out the meaning of this vision. The fascinating question is just why God chooses to favour those taken away to wicked Babylon (vs 4–7) and not the remnant who remain at home (vs 8–10). The answer is not entirely clear, and this is a good occasion on which to acknowledge the principle that God is sovereign. His understanding is total, and his purpose is entirely good. However, his response here does tie in with other times when it is evident that God deals more readily with a complete brokenness, followed by a fresh, new start, rather than a bodging-up of human plans. There is a message here for us if we are inclined to cling to crumbling remains of past comforts when our Lord is telling us to properly move on.

'My eyes will watch over them for their good, and I will bring them back to this land. I will build them up and not tear them down.'
Jeremiah 24:6

RESPOND
Ask the Lord to show you whether you retain, in your spiritual life, habits or ideas which are no longer enriching, either for you or for his church.

. . . .

Bible in a year: Jeremiah 47,48; John 17

Thursday 27 October
Jeremiah 25:1–29

Listening skills

PREPARE
Make a list of times when you believe God has spoken to you in some way. Do you see any pattern?

....

READ
Jeremiah 25:1–29

EXPLORE
The business of listening comes up four times early in chapter 25. In each case, people are not listening to God. There are valuable lessons for us here. First, we read (v 3) that for many years Jeremiah has been proclaiming God's word. Is it possible that his listeners became over-familiar with prophetic warnings so that the message washed over them? Could it be that they (and we) fail to properly 'pay attention' (v 4)? There is a real challenge in listening to God. It involves a cost for us in terms of time and perhaps in focusing away from our preferred everyday concerns. Part of the problem – for me at any rate – is that listening to words can seem ephemeral. It is not like baking a cake or building a wall. And, to add to our struggles, God does often seem to speak in ways which we might not have chosen ourselves – such as the Book of Jeremiah...

Let us be warned. If we don't take care to listen, we may well find ourselves being force-fed (vs 27,28). The latter sections of this chapter comprise a terrible account of the out-working of God's righteous anger. Because he is gracious, and loves us, he has given us fair warning of his purpose.

> ... the word of the LORD has come to me and I have spoken to you again and again, but you have not listened.
>
> **Jeremiah 25:3**

RESPOND
Ask God to refresh your listening skills so that you may hear from him through his Word, his people and his Spirit.

....

Bible in a year: Jeremiah 49,50; John 18

Tell it how it is

PREPARE
In what situation would you be most afraid to proclaim the gospel? Imagine yourself in that place.

....

READ
Jeremiah 26:1–24

EXPLORE
Look back to Jeremiah 1:4–8. When Jeremiah is called to be a prophet, his response is, 'I am only a child.' Yet here he is now, apparently alone, standing before the very seat of power, threatening the religious leaders themselves with destruction. The account is vivid: what courage it takes to look dangerous men in the eye and speak the truth. For a time, it must have seemed to Jeremiah that his time was up (vs 14,15). Then, no doubt prompted by the Holy Spirit, good people like Ahikam (v 24) stepped in to save the day. What we cannot know is how Jeremiah felt personally. He is the same 'child' as in chapter 1, but the tone of verse 14 suggests that he is entirely reconciled to his fate, at peace in God's hands. This accords with Jesus' words in Luke 12:11,12. If ever we find ourselves in a place anything like this, one thing we can be assured of is the Lord's presence and support.

Verse 3 is striking. God himself says to Jeremiah, 'Perhaps'. Just possibly, the people will repent. The mystery of our omnipotent God and his gracious wish that we might change is at the very heart of the mystery of our faith.

> 'Tell them everything I command you; do not omit a word.'
>
> **Jeremiah 26:2**

RESPOND
Pray that we might find situations in which to speak God's truth – and that the Holy Spirit will give us the words to say.

....

Bible in a year: Jeremiah 51,52; Psalm 119:73–96

God knows what he's doing

PREPARE

Which nation in our times do you think God is most pleased with?

....

READ

Jeremiah 27:1–22

EXPLORE

It is good to ask two questions about any portion of scripture. What can we learn? And what should we then do? I do not know exactly why God prompted Jeremiah to make a yoke and wear it at an international conference. I am not clear why he concerned himself with these particular ancient kings and kingdoms. Even with the benefit of hindsight, I do not really understand why God's purpose was for Babylon to subjugate Judah and all the other nations (v 7). And, in all honesty, left to my own devices, the destiny of the Temple furnishings (v 19) would not have troubled me overmuch.

Ancient Scriptures are sometimes baffling. However, my puzzlement is not important. These are not sentences about which we are asked to form opinions. This is the holy Word of God, given to us for our benefit and to his glory. One key thing which we can learn – or

be reminded of – is that God is in control. His righteous plan is the one which is declared here, and it involves the whole of humanity, with repercussions echoing down the ages. One thing we can do, as our own age reels in turmoil around us, can be found in verse 11. Thank God if we can '… remain in our own land … to live there'. Then we are very fortunate people, and God would not want us to forget it.

> 'But if any nation will bow its neck under the yoke of the king of Babylon and serve him, I will let that nation remain in its own land to till it and to live there…'
>
> **Jeremiah 27:11**

RESPOND

Pray for the rulers of the great nations of the twenty-first century.

....

Bible in a year: Lamentations 1,2; John 19

Never the end of the story

PREPARE
Pray now for someone you know, or know of, who is responsible for the persecution and suffering of others (see Matthew 5:44).

....

READ
Psalm 69

EXPLORE

There is nothing like the psalms. All emotional life is here. Psalm 69 is one in which a human soul exposes itself utterly. Apologies if you turned from rather heavy Jeremiah readings this Sunday hoping for a gentle, pastoral psalm. This is not one of those.

The roller-coaster ride which is Psalm 69 begins with the cry, 'Save me'. Many bleak images paint a picture of someone at the very end of their hope and their resource. To make matters worse, there are enemies planning the writer's death and – to some extent – it is the writer who is to blame (v 5). Staring up from these depths, it is astonishing that the psalmist is able, in verse 13, to write (or sing) of the 'great love' and the 'sure salvation' of the same Lord whom we Christians serve.

Weirdly, verses 22–28 then shift straight into a horrible, cursing mode. How on earth are we to reconcile this with the lovely final, celebratory section? Let's be as clear as Jesus was: this outpouring of bitterness is not OK (Matthew 5:44). However, it is real, it is human, and, by the end of the psalm, it is dealt with. The grim sections of the Bible are never the end of the story.

> But as for me, afflicted and in pain – may your salvation, God, protect me.
>
> **Psalm 69:29**

RESPOND
Ask the Lord to expose the darkest places of our hearts so that we, too, might find the mercy proclaimed in verse 16.

....

Bible in a year: Lamentations 3–5; John 20

Monday 31 October
Jeremiah 28:1–17

Whom should we trust?

PREPARE
Bring to mind a few people whom you completely trust. What is it about them?

. . . .

READ
Jeremiah 28:1–17

EXPLORE
Suppose that you were someone fresh on the scene listening to this discussion between two supposed prophets. How on earth were you to know who was telling the truth: who was a genuine prophet of the Lord? It is clear that the country was awash with people claiming to be prophets in Jeremiah's days (see Jeremiah chapter 14). The culture is very different in our times but still we are bombarded – including online – by those who claim to have *the* answer to life's complex, intractable problems.

A sound scriptural principle, outlined in 1 John 4:1, is that we should 'test the spirits'. Those listening to Jeremiah and Hananiah would have done well to apply the idea. They might have learned, from experience and relationship, who those individuals are whom we can trust. This account does not come at the beginning of Jeremiah's ministry. Many of those watching really should have known that Jeremiah was a true servant of God whose word was to be trusted and should have advised others. This is true even though Hananiah was telling the people what they wanted to hear. A second method of testing is simple. Jeremiah could afford to walk away (in verse 11) because he knew that his words and not the other person's would come true.

> 'But the prophet who prophesies peace will be recognised as one truly sent by the Lord only if his prediction comes true.'
> **Jeremiah 28:9**

RESPOND
Ask God to grow your relationships with true friends. Pray that those people might speak into your life.

. . . .

Bible in a year: Ezekiel 1; John 21

Letter of hope

PREPARE
Call to mind the promises God has made to you.

....

READ
Jeremiah 29:1–23

EXPLORE
Today's reading centres, unusually, around a letter written by Jeremiah to the exiles in Babylon – and it's a wonderful one. Jeremiah's message might properly be called an 'epistle': a significant, formal letter to a group of people with the purpose of uplifting their spirits, strengthening their resolve not to be led astray, and affirming their destiny as people of God.

We are reminded that, for whatever reason, God's favour rests not upon those who have remained behind but with the exiles. It is clear (v 7) that God intends Babylon to flourish for this time, while the Israelites are living there. The Lord's kingdom is not firstly about a location but about a people. Perhaps verse 14 is a for-all-time prophecy about the spiritual gathering, which he has promised, of God's dispersed people. It is because he cares for his own children so much that his anger is so great against those who would lead them astray (v 16) and deliberately lie to them (v 21). But the glorious heart of Jeremiah's letter is the promise God makes (vs 10–14). Notice the homely details in verses 5–7. This letter is not firstly about people sinning or repenting or obeying. It's much more an expression of the intimate connection between God and his people in love and trust.

'For I know the plans I have for you,' declares the Lord, 'plans to prosper you and not to harm you, plans to give you hope and a future.'
Jeremiah 29:11

RESPOND
Do you still write letters? Why not write one today, encouraging a fellow Christian by sharing this eternal promise from the Lord?

....

Bible in a year: Ezekiel 2,3; Psalm 119:97–120

Wednesday 2 November
Jeremiah 30:1–24

Hope of deliverance

PREPARE
Pray for the Lord's involvement in our world, in the threats of climate change, pandemics, terrorism and Godless immorality.

....

READ
Jeremiah 30:1–24

EXPLORE
There is now a shift in mood. To be sure, the next few chapters still include the standard Jeremiah cheeriness such as 'How awful that day...' (v 7) and 'Your wound is incurable' (v 12). However, now these realities are held verse by verse within a brighter vision of hope to come. All the history of God's covenants is embodied here, as expressed in his relationships with Abraham, Moses and others. (See, for example, Deuteronomy 30:1–10.)

Jeremiah's scribe and editor is someone called Baruch (eg Jeremiah 32:8–16; 36). His lines of connected reasoning here do not fall into modern patterns – which is fair enough (I am not sure I would like to explain Facebook to Baruch!). In this chapter, his points seem to flow in a bewildering sort of bad news/good news succession. However, a key idea is that, invariably, God's deliverance is promised. Look out for the following: restoration in verse 3; salvation in verse 7; protection in verse 11; justice and healing in verses 16 and 17; thanksgiving for reconstruction in verse 18; the full accomplishment of God's purposes in verse 24. There is even the promise that one day we will understand, for which I, at any rate, will be grateful.

'So you will be my people, and I will be your God.'

Jeremiah 30:22

RESPOND
Thank God for his mastery of all those grim situations about which, just now, we can hear nothing from him, whether these are personal or in the wider world.

....

Bible in a year: Ezekiel 4,5; James 1

God sees the future

PREPARE
Read verses 2–4 several times out loud to yourself. You might like to use the Authorised Version for this.

. . . .

READ
Jeremiah 31:1–40

EXPLORE
This is one of the most beautiful chapters in the Bible. Its over-riding theme is the outworking of the love of God for his people. This idea is practically and literally inexpressible. Jeremiah, therefore, chooses to convey it through layer after layer of rich, beguiling imagery. Some of the points, such as in verse 5, may be describing actual events. Others may be metaphorical: from verse 9 we might wonder whether Jeremiah has read Psalm 23! Does it matter on this occasion whether these images are literally or metaphorically true? I would suggest not. Through his prophet, God himself is celebrating and asking us to share his joy in the time, now come, when he can be reunited with his children. Anyone who suggests that this book is all doom and gloom should be asked to consider all the affirmations in this chapter. I count well over 50.

It is characteristic of Jeremiah that, in verse 15, the mood shifts briefly to utmost grief. Again, we might think of the literal biblical character of Rachel, mother of Joseph, or Rachel as a symbolic representative of motherhood. (Note that the reading includes diverse masculine and feminine images.) At any rate, here, once again God declares, as only he can, hope for the future.

'The days are coming,' declares the LORD, 'when I will make a new covenant with the people of Israel and with the people of Judah.'

Jeremiah 31:31

RESPOND
Verse 34 tells us that God has forgotten altogether about our sins. How do you propose to celebrate?

. . . .

Bible in a year: Ezekiel 6,7; James 2

Just do as you are told

PREPARE
Ask the Holy Spirit to speak to you in fresh ways and to make you attentive to his guidance however it comes.

••

READ
Jeremiah 32:1–15

EXPLORE
We find ourselves now in the dark, final days for Judah, with Jerusalem surrounded and Jeremiah a prisoner in the besieged city. King Zedekiah is totally intransigent. Even at the very last, the last king will not hear God's word, preferring to lock up the true prophet. With Babylonian arrows flying and Israelite families starving, it seems an odd moment at which to focus on the details of an apparently pointless land purchase. However, God did sometimes inspire his prophets to perform symbolic enactments of his purposes in addition to spoken and written words. Remember the potter's jar (chapter 19) and the yoke bars (chapter 27). For Jeremiah, at any rate, it was enough to know that ' … this was the word of the LORD,' (v 8), and he did exactly as instructed.

It was the ancient custom to store important documents in clay jars. The famous Dead Sea Scrolls were discovered well preserved after they had been stored in this way for 2,000 years. The point is clear. The deed of purchase given to Baruch is intended as a permanent record (vs 12–15). To the desperate survivors in the city, this might have seemed a meaningless document. To those still trusting in God's word, and his deeds, this purchase of land is an act of faith: God's covenant with his people is for ever.

'For this is what the LORD Almighty, the God of Israel, says: houses, fields and vineyards will again be bought in this land.'
Jeremiah 32:15

RESPOND
Pray for those in refugee camps, who feel no hope for the future today.

••

Bible in a year: Ezekiel 8,9; Psalm 119:121–144

The prophet's prayer

PREPARE
Spend some time telling the Lord God what he is like and what he has done.

. . . .

READ
Jeremiah 32:16–27

EXPLORE
Jeremiah has acted in good faith. He has continued to proclaim God's word – that Judah should surrender to Babylon – in spite of the fact that no one was willing to hear it. He has followed God's guidance, even though it did not seem to make much sense. Verse 25 is fascinating. Jeremiah points out to God that he has followed his instructions, even though the city and the land are on the very cusp of being conquered. One delight of this book is that we really do get to know Jeremiah as a human being. God, loving him, seems to allow Jeremiah to imply, 'What on earth's the point?' (v 25) – and we can surely see why.

This (verses 17–25) is a great prayer in many ways. First, consider the context. We can only imagine Jeremiah's physical circumstances, imprisoned by his own compatriots in the dying city (32:2). Now, very likely at the end of his practical and spiritual resources, the prophet chooses to pray. Only in the last section does Jeremiah speak of his and his nation's current calamity. Instead, most of the prayer is a powerful recollection of God's eternal nature, his power and his bounty. There is a lesson here for us. At times, we might wonder what to pray. We can always speak of God's goodness and love.

'Ah, Sovereign LORD, you have made the heavens and the earth by your great power and outstretched arm. Nothing is too hard for you.'
Jeremiah 32:17

RESPOND
Bring to mind some of the disasters of our own age, and affirm that God *will* resolve each one.

. . . .

Bible in a year: Ezekiel 10,11; James 3

Hurry up, God!

PREPARE
How long should you reasonably wait before your prayers are answered?

. . . .

READ
Psalm 70

EXPLORE
One of the disconnects between us and our God is to do with time. The Almighty dwells in eternity and oversees the full picture. We bumble along day by day, indeed often counting the days until our adversaries are displaced and put to 'shame and confusion' (v 2). I don't suppose there has ever been a believer who has not called upon God to 'hasten': to move us quickly past our current woes and into the safe space, the place of contentment that we instinctively sense should be just up ahead. Why does God so often seem to prefer time scales beyond our understanding? Come on, Lord! What's the delay?

Perhaps I would not dare to type that unless I had just read verse 5. The great thing about the psalmists is that they are never afraid to declare to God precisely how they feel. One reason for the boldness of the writers is that they are, in several respects, in the right place. Their very first words here are a cry to God. They readily acknowledge their own lowliness and God's greatness. They clearly count themselves among those in verse 4, those on the Lord's side. It is in this role, as God's servant, that the psalmist feels able to ask for God's support in putting down the adversaries described in verses 2 and 3.

> But as for me, I am poor and needy; come quickly to me, O God. You are my help and my deliverer; LORD, do not delay.
>
> **Psalm 70:5**

RESPOND
Tell the Lord now that whatever happens, you are on his side today.

. . . .

Bible in a year: Ezekiel 12,13; James 4

Ancient, new and for ever

PREPARE
How would you compare the God of the Old Testament with the one we know from the Gospels?

READ
Jeremiah 33:1–26

EXPLORE
Here is a shocking contrast. On the one hand, we have the besieged city in its final days. Great buildings are demolished, dead bodies lie untended, and, in the city prison, the prophet Jeremiah languishes (vs 1–5). On the other hand, from within the soul of that prisoner, presumably starving, filthy and grieving, comes a vision of the good and all-powerful God and of the wonders he will bring to pass. Jeremiah must have achieved a profound connection with his Lord in order to see in this way beyond his squalid personal circumstances.

His insights on divine nature and attributes are striking. God is not only the creator but also the teacher, the healer, the source of blessing, the builder, the one who cleanses from sin, the restorer, the provider of all good things, the one who, above all, loves his people. See if you can find these attributes in verses 3–11. One remarkable aspect of these godly features, cited by Jeremiah, is how alike they are to the God explained in the New Testament, by Jesus or Paul. We find a God of grace (v 14), salvation (v 16) and compassion (v 26). The worldly kingdom he set up is, in everyday terms, about to fall into ruin. In deeper and truer terms, his reign, through David's son, will never end (v 17).

> 'Give thanks to the LORD Almighty, for the LORD is good; his love endures for ever.'
>
> **Jeremiah 33:11**

RESPOND
Pray for the modern nation of Israel, that its people may finally come to know Jesus.

Bible in a year: Ezekiel 14,15; James 5

Tuesday 8 November
Jeremiah 34:1–22

A rather ordinary man

PREPARE
On what basis should we judge our political leaders? Bring to mind a few whom you consider the best and the worst.

. . . .

READ
Jeremiah 34:1–22

EXPLORE
Several aspects of this fascinating chapter are unclear. The end of Zedekiah's dismal reign approaches (vs 21,22) – more grisly details can be found in Jeremiah chapter 52. On the other hand, we find here God's promise, to someone he loves, that Zedekiah's last days will be spent in peace and honour (vs 4,5). How so? One idea is that this Hebrew word for 'promise' (v 4: *dabar*) implies conditionality, and Zedekiah blatantly ignored God's conditions.* Another thought is that, even as a blinded, grieving prisoner, this man could indeed have found a final peace with his Lord. Let's hope so – this young leader was dealing with appalling circumstances.

The other story in this chapter, to do with slaves, is also not simple.* It seems from verse 8 that Zedekiah was instrumental in proclaiming the release of slaves – though why, we do not know (but see Exodus 21:1–11; Deuteronomy 15:12–15). Verse 11 tells us that 'the officials' were the ones to then force people back into slavery. Probably by this stage, the king's grip on events in his dwindling territory was less than firm. That said, it is clear from verses 12–14 that God's original covenant is no less applicable just because times are tough.

> '... the LORD, the God of Israel, says: go to Zedekiah king of Judah and tell him ... I am about to give this city into the hands of the king of Babylon...'
>
> **Jeremiah 34:2**

RESPOND
Thankfully, it is not for us to judge Zedekiah. Rather, let's give thanks that we can receive mercy rather than justice at the hands of God.

*See also Christopher Wright, *The Message of Jeremiah*, IVP (2014), 356–363.

. . . .

Bible in a year: Ezekiel 16,17; Psalm 119:145–176

"I DON'T GO TO CHURCH BUT..."

95% of under-18s don't go to church. **BUT** many are open to faith.

Together we can reach them!

SCAN TO JOIN THE 95 CAMPAIGN FOR FREE

The Gospels

Our starting point as we approach the books of Matthew, Mark, Luke and John is to understand the aim and purpose of these books. Why were they written? Are they biographies? Are they meant to be read as historical accounts? Why are there four accounts that seem to have discrepancies between them, with the Gospel of John being so different from the others (eg only John has the 'I am' sayings)?

Today, it's common to view the Gospels as biographies of Jesus. Helen Bond's book on Mark, *The First Biography of Jesus*,* represents the consensus. But let's not imagine that the Gospels are exactly like modern biographies, providing a chronological and objective account of the subjects. Ancient biographies did not intend to present a strict chronological account and were written to highlight their subjects as role models and to promote their teaching. None of this implies the Gospel writers made up stories or were unconcerned about presenting an accurate record. Richard Bauckham's *Jesus and the Eyewitnesses*** provides a robust argument for the Gospels being based on eyewitness accounts, meant to be read as real-life events.

Why were they written? If the writers are not seeking to be strictly chronological and unbiased, what is their intention? Thomas Merton comments, 'The teaching and miracles of Christ were not meant simply to draw attention to a doctrine or set of practices' but 'to focus our attention upon God himself revealed in the person of Jesus Christ.'*** Each Gospel writer brings their own perspective, skilfully moulding the material they have gathered to focus us on Jesus, and we must discern what each particularly wants to teach us about him.

Clearly, Matthew, Mark and Luke are much more alike, containing many of the same stories and teaching. That's why they are called the 'synoptic Gospels', 'synoptic' meaning 'seeing or viewing together'. They build the story of Jesus as the growing discovery of his identity, gradually unveiling the truth about who he is. From the very start, however, John reveals Jesus as eternal, the creator, the source of life. His account provides us with signs (miracles) that display this revelation.

Whatever the starting point, the focus is primarily on the person of Jesus, but also on *the response* of the disciples, the crowds and the religious and secular authorities to Jesus. We, too, have to decide: Will we accept and follow this Jesus? Will we say with Peter, 'Lord, to whom shall we go? You have the words of eternal life' (John 6:68)?

As we read the Gospels, it's worth reflecting on...

What are the different themes or emphases of these books? It helps to read the whole book through before getting into the detail. Notice: Matthew's emphasis on fulfilment of Old Testament promises and God's kingdom; Mark's concern to show the sovereign power of Jesus; Luke's interest in Jesus and women, prayer and possessions; and John's focus on the signs and 'I am' sayings.

Let the story speak. Much of the content of the Gospels is in the form of story or narrative. Think your way into the story, perhaps even imagining yourself as a bystander or a character in the story. What would you see? What would you think?

Don't move too quickly to the lesson of the story or immediately try to fit it into your theological system!

Notice the context. None of the stories or teaching exist in isolation. The author always has a reason for where he places them. For example, when Matthew places Herod's beheading of John the Baptist next to Jesus' feeding of the 5,000 in Matthew 14, is he intending to contrast Herod's abuse of power with Jesus using his power to bless people?

Compare the stories across the Gospels. They have different standpoints, which can at times cause us difficulties. You won't resolve all of these, but ask yourself: How does this different perspective contribute to a better understanding of the Lord Jesus?

The last few days of Jesus are given the most space in all the Gospels. That's a guide to us for where to focus our own reflection.

Writer: Andy Bathgate

Useful resources
The First Biography of Jesus, Helen K Bond, Eerdmans (2020).
***Jesus and the Eyewitnesses*, Richard Bauckham, Eerdmans (2006); also *The Gospels as Eyewitness Testimony*, Grove Books 1 (2008).
****No Man is an Island*, Thomas Merton, Burns and Oates (1961), p 163.
How to Read the Gospel, The Bible Project, https://www.youtube.com/watch?v=xrzq_X1NNaA

Dying to self

'As the time approached for him to be taken up to heaven…' (Luke 9:51), Jesus heads for Jerusalem, to his death for the sins of the whole world. And this is only chapter 9 of 24 in Luke! Yes, the Gospel story is mostly about this.

Yet Jesus isn't focused on his death but on the joy ('heaven') that lies beyond. That has to be right for us too, doesn't it, if we're following Jesus? So, there's no panic or desperation in Jesus but a deep sense of purpose (as in John 13:1–5, when Jesus, knowing he's about to die, picks up a towel and starts washing his disciples' feet).

Following Jesus means living a life focused on sacrifice – on the generous giving of ourselves – not on selfish gain. It is about 'dying to self' – for us not physically dying but asking for Jesus' help to deal a death blow to selfishness.

I've been following Jesus for decades. You'd think I'd know what it's all about by now! But as we travel with Jesus on the way up to Jerusalem, I'm going to commit to letting his words and actions challenge my understanding about what it means to follow him. Will you join me? It won't be a comfortable journey, but I so long to be doing the right thing for the right reasons, don't you? Knowing there's nowhere I'd rather be than close to Jesus, and nothing I'd rather be doing than living the way he wants me to?

About the writer
Terry Clutterham

Once a staff member of the publishing, content and leadership teams of SU England and Wales, Terry now lives with his wife Sue in Norfolk, where they enjoy exploring the countryside, reading, writing, and discovering how God might use them in their new church in Norwich.

Jesus above all else

PREPARE
Speak with Jesus about your motivation for following him. Is it just about being friends with the One who can make things happen the way you want them to? Well, what *is* it about then?

· ·

READ
Luke 9:51–62

EXPLORE
The Samaritans aren't going to help *anyone* get to Jerusalem (vs 52,53), the religious and cultural centre of the Jews they despise so much. 'So let's burn them up, Jesus!' his headstrong disciples advise (v 54), thinking the Samaritans deserve it and knowing that Jesus can easily do it. 'Let's not,' says Jesus, maybe thinking that he's come to save Samaritans too (John 4:39–42) and knowing that their destruction is *not* what a life of selfless sacrifice looks like.

Now enter three guys who seem to be doing the right thing – thinking seriously about following Jesus. The first (v 57) is eager and committed enough but maybe just wants to do the popular, 'cool' thing and doesn't realise there'll be a high price to pay. The second (vs 59,60) learns that Jesus must come first – it's no good wanting to sort out life first, including family, and then maybe

one day getting round to following Jesus. And for the third (vs 61,62), Jesus knows that emotional family farewells might indicate someone whose heart will never totally be his.

Jesus replied, 'No one who puts a hand to the plough and looks back is fit for service in the kingdom of God.'
Luke 9:62

RESPOND
These verses are easy enough as long as they're about these three guys – but suppose they're also about *us* following Jesus? That makes them much harder to take, if we really think about it.

· ·

Bible in a year: Ezekiel 18,19; 1 Peter 1

Unsurprising setbacks

PREPARE

'Let my heart want for only you; let my heart want for nothing but you, just you' (from 'Only Jesus', © 2016 Bethel Music, by Jason Ingram, Brian Johnson, Hank Bentley and Joel Taylor).

READ

Luke 10:1–16

EXPLORE

Following Jesus means having the same priorities he has and living the life he lives. It's inseparable togetherness for ever (John 14:20). Just as he's constantly on a mission to bring people to God, so are we. That's exactly what he asks his followers to pray for (v 2) – *we* are some of those much-needed 'workers'.

And on this tough, urgent mission, following a Saviour who goes to a horrid death before rising to life again means that we too can anticipate hardship, pain, opposition and a feeling of helplessness, while we also look forward to fruitfulness and victory. That's all part of 'dying to self', and it's normal – lambs can't expect much fun from a pack of wolves (v 3).

People have always rejected God and his ways, and they always will. Remember Sodom – the problem (Genesis 18:20,21) and the outcome (Genesis 19:24)? The towns of Chorazin and Bethsaida (v 13) had Jesus himself bless them with miracles, but in the end, they were too wrapped up in themselves. Even Capernaum – where for a while Jesus lived, taught and healed people – couldn't care less about him (v 15).

> 'Go! I am sending you out like lambs among wolves.'
>
> **Luke 10:3**

RESPOND

Sometimes, as we follow Jesus, our hearts will be broken when we bring good news to those closest to us and they reject it – sometimes us too. Pour out to Jesus any heartbreak like this that you have experienced.

Bible in a year: Ezekiel 20,21; 1 Peter 2

Real joy

PREPARE

Recall a time recently when God used you to bring blessing into someone's life. Reflect on the privilege it is to be involved in what Jesus is still doing on earth – giving Satan a really hard time!

· ·

READ

Luke 10:17–24

EXPLORE

On today's leg of the journey, there are two surprising and challenging insights from Jesus about what it means to follow him. First, even though he warned his 72 disciples of the possible hardships and setbacks ahead of them (vs 3,10,16), they're coming back overwhelmingly successful in their mission (v 17). They're laughing! But how lasting is the source of their joy?

'Rejoicing in the Lord means knowing Jesus Christ as our Lord, Saviour and Treasure. It means he gives us deeper, purer, sweeter, more lasting pleasure and gladness than anything this world has to offer' (Brian Tabb in 'Rejoice even though'*) – even all the wonderful things he does through us. Is this true for me?

Secondly, what the 72 have just learned fills Jesus with joy (v 21). As 'ordinary' as they are, they've grasped and experienced the mystery of knowing God through Jesus. No one before them has had this privilege (v 24). Though not exactly in the same way as those first followers, I should be amazed every day that I too – ordinary me – have come to know and experience him. How can I prompt myself about this?

'No one knows who the Son is except the Father, and no one knows who the Father is except the Son and those to whom the Son chooses to reveal him.'

Luke 10:22b

RESPOND

'Rejoice! Rejoice! Christ is in you, the hope of glory in our hearts'.**

---

*https://www.desiringgod.org/articles/rejoice-even-though
*'Rejoice!', Graham Kendrick, © 1983, Thankyou Music.

· ·

Bible in a year: Ezekiel 22,23; Psalms 120–122

Selflessness

PREPARE

Use Psalm 107:1,2 as inspiration to thank God for all the good things he has brought into your life.

· ·

READ

Luke 10:25–37

EXPLORE

In a way, Jesus doesn't really need to say anything after the lawyer's answer (v 27). It captures exactly the purpose of the story that follows … except the lawyer doesn't get the 'neighbour' part.

This is what discipleship is all about – responding to God's grace and goodness with all of ourselves, all we think, say, feel and do – and letting our thankfulness spill over into the way we treat others. If we could only love perfectly, that's all that would be needed – Jesus needn't continue with the story. But we can't because we're blinkered and sinful – essentially, selfish and self-preserving.

It's not about how much we have to do to earn a way into God's good books, as the lawyer thinks (v 25). The story Jesus tells (vs 30–35) shows there can be no limits or exceptions to this thankful way of living. The focus is not on how much

we need to do, or should or should not do (as the two religious leaders thought), but on how much *our 'neighbour'* needs (as the Samaritan demonstrates selflessly). Following Jesus means being so thankful to God that we don't even stop to think about how much serving others is costing us. This too is part of 'dying to self'.

He answered, 'Love the Lord your God with all your heart and with all your soul and with all your strength and with all you mind'; and, 'Love your neighbour as yourself.'

Luke 10:27

RESPOND

So, what happens now, when Jesus says to *you*, 'Go and do likewise' (v 37)?

· ·

Bible in a year: Ezekiel 24,25; 1 Peter 3

Snapshots

PREPARE
Confession time. I may be just a little obsessive about keeping my digital photo albums up to date and in order. How careful are *you* about keeping good memories?

· ·

READ
Psalm 71

EXPLORE
Today's psalm, written by an older person, is a like a series of snapshots from the life of a God-follower, except the images are a bit fuzzy. We don't really know what these moments were, but read the verse(s) again and use them as prompts for praise, prayer and thanks to God. And let them strengthen your faith for any tough time you're going through just now (vs 1–4). Essentially, psalms help us worship.

Verses 5–8. Remember the early days of your life of faith, and thank God for the ways he has led and protected you since then. When, particularly, did he give you 'hope' and 'confidence'?

Verses 9–16. Discipleship means following God with all that we are, for as long as we live. Pray that he will keep you close to him for ever and your life will always be a strong and faithful witness to his goodness.

Verses 17–21. What better to leave 'the next generation' than a good understanding of how powerful God is? Pray that you'll be so full of the good news of Jesus that you won't be able to help but pass it on. But to whom? That's the question. Do you know yet?

> As for me, I shall always have hope; I will praise you more and more.
>
> **Psalm 71:14**

RESPOND
Verses 22–24. Look forward thankfully for all the Lord has in store for you in heaven, and get ready for plenty of singing to him!

· ·

Bible in a year: Ezekiel 26,27; 1 Peter 4

Focus on what's better

PREPARE

Understanding the Bible and responding to it require God's help – we can't do it on our own. Ask the Lord to help you get in tune with what he wants to say to you today.

. . . .

READ
Luke 10:38–42

EXPLORE

Christians are notoriously busy people – often *too* busy. Church-organised activities and the many needs of family, friends, neighbours and various good causes prompt us to do more and more. But we know from Saturday's reading that we can't earn our way into God's good books, and we may find we're doing all these things at the expense of time to pray and hear from God.

At Martha's home, Jesus prompts us to ask the question, 'Exactly how much do we *need* to do?' And his answer is 'less' (see v 42). Jesus doesn't say exactly what the 'only one' thing is that's needed, but somehow it relates to the time Mary spends hanging on Jesus' words, wholly dependent on him.

Someone once said to me, 'If you've got too much to do and too little time to do it, be sure you're doing something God doesn't want.' That certainly made me sit up and think. To be honest, it's still a challenge for me to sit still, keep quiet and listen to him, but I'm trying. Do you read the Bible and pray with *Daily Bread* when you have time to linger, or is it always a rush? Do you need to rethink?

'Mary has chosen what is better, and it will not be taken away from her.'

Luke 10:42b

RESPOND

'Speak, Lord, in the stillness while I wait on thee; hushed my heart to listen in expectancy' (Emily Crawford, 1920).

. . . .

Bible in a year: Ezekiel 28,29; 1 Peter 5

Dependence

PREPARE

'Disciples' means 'learners'. Disciples of Jesus know they've never learned enough, never 'arrived'. Declare to God your hunger to learn from him now.

READ

Luke 11:1–4

EXPLORE

Disciples also know they're not the centre of the universe – God is – and everything and everyone depends entirely on him. 'Dying to self' involves giving up any sense of being independent. Prayer expresses this dependence. Pray Jesus' words as they are ('When you pray, say...' v 2), or use them as a model for your prayer ('This, then, is how you should pray...' Matthew 6:9).

'Father' (v 2). It's all about you, Lord, just you. Our origin, roots, place of belonging; the One from whom we've received life and will inherit every good thing.

'Hallowed be your name' (v 2). We long for everyone to acknowledge how great you are – this is our life goal.

'Your kingdom come' (v 2). If only you ruled in *everyone's* heart, Father – this is our desire. Please. *Please.*

'Give us each day our daily bread' (v 3). You give us everything we need, Father – every hour, day, month, year. All we are depends on you.

'Forgive us our sins' (v 4). Only through Jesus is this possible. We can only look to you, Lord.

'And lead us not into temptation' (v 4). Help us, Father, to keep from all that risks drawing us away from you. In ourselves we're too weak, but you are our strength.

... 'When you pray, say: "Father, hallowed be your name, your kingdom come."'

Luke 11:2

RESPOND

'You're my all, you're the best; you're my joy, my righteousness, and I love you, Lord'.*

*'Knowing You', Graham Kendrick, © 1993, Make Way Music.

Bible in a year: Ezekiel 30,31; Psalms 123–125

Wednesday 16 November
Luke 11:5–13

Great expectations

PREPARE
Thank God for any prayers he has answered recently, and bring to him any that you seem to have been praying for a long time, so far without seeing an answer.

READ
Luke 11:5–13

EXPLORE
Sometimes I'm so slow to learn because I'm so quick to forget. Take these two stories Jesus tells. First (vs 5–8), there's something I've been praying for, for a very long time, but nothing has changed. So, I stop and immediately start to think, 'What's wrong with God?' Pretty arrogant of me? Sure. Really, I should be listening at that moment. It's then that our Father is asking, 'How much do you want this, and how much do you trust me?' As William Hendriksen said:

'With God it is never midnight; he never lacks anything; he is never "bothered" when any humble child approaches him; and he is never taken by surprise.'*

Secondly (vs 9–13), why am I ever disappointed in answers to prayer? It's not as if God gets it wrong, like some poorly chosen Christmas gift. Even 'no' should be a cause for rejoicing, simply because he knows what's best! And of course, he has already given us the Holy Spirit to bring all the good news God has to offer into our lives. What's not to like?

'So I say to you: ask and it will be given to you; seek and you will find; knock and the door will be opened to you.'
Luke 11:9

RESPOND
Take a moment to examine your own attitude to prayer before God. Is there anything we need to be sorry about? Anything we really need to persevere in prayer about? As disciples, we'll always need to go round the learning loop one more time.

*William Hendriksen, *The Gospel of Luke*, The Banner of Truth Trust, © 1978

Bible in a year: Ezekiel 32,33; 2 Peter 1

Reassurance

PREPARE

Have you ever witnessed a miracle first-hand? If so, what was your reaction? Praise, bewilderment, amazement, fear, scepticism? Or has God ever used you to bring a miracle into someone's life? How did others react?

READ

Luke 11:14–28

EXPLORE

Religious leaders (according to Matthew 12:24 and Mark 3:22) pile into Jesus with hatred. He's more popular and powerful than they are, and he doesn't keep their traditions (vs 15,16). They won't accept he's from God, but everyone can see he's doing amazing things. So, they'd better discredit him by claiming he's in partnership with Satan (Beelzebul, v 15) – at least that will explain where his power comes from.

As followers of Jesus, we know that being on his side doesn't mean an easy life for us either. It can make people wary of us, suspicious of our motives and sceptical about the reality of God at work. But Jesus assures us that we're on the winning side in the battle of the two kingdoms – Satan's and God's. Jesus is undoubtedly the 'someone stronger' (v 22), and we're with *him*.

When God comes and 'cleans up' a person's life, he doesn't leave it barren, empty and useless – otherwise the empty doesn't stay empty for long (vs 24–26)! Instead, he fills it with good, and the good overflows to others. In whom have you seen this happen when they became a Christian?

> 'Whoever is not with me is against me, and whoever does not gather with me scatters.'
>
> **Luke 11:23**

RESPOND

Praise God for the reassurance Romans 8:31–39 gives us. Pray that your life will always provide clear evidence that God is good and most powerful.

Bible in a year: Ezekiel 34,35; 2 Peter 2

Friday 18 November
Luke 11:29–36

Lighten up

PREPARE

'I am the light of the world. Whoever follows me will never walk in darkness, but will have the light of life' (John 8:12). Use Psalm 18:28 to help you praise and thank God for bringing light into your life through Jesus.

. . . .

READ
Luke 11:29–36

EXPLORE

When Jesus is raised to life again, that will be evidence that all he's saying is true (v 30), just as the people of Nineveh were convinced when Jonah reappeared out of the fish after three days (Jonah 1:17; 3:5). Who'll need more? So, Jesus isn't about to produce 'signs' on demand – after all, he has already done the miracle for the demon-possessed man (v 14), and people still aren't getting it (v 16). One day, his resurrection will be enough. People will then see the light.

Jesus is challenging his listeners about where they stand in relation to him: are they focused on doing and being good, oriented towards pleasing God or on doing and being evil, focused on themselves (v 34)? That's the choice everyone has to make in life, and the job of Jesus' followers is to help them consider Jesus and make the best choice – for *him*. One way we can help them see the reality and goodness of God is by demonstrating the fruit of the Spirit in our daily lives (Galatians 5:22,23).

'See to it, then, that the light within you is not darkness.'
Luke 11:35

RESPOND
Think about how the Holy Spirit enables you to show each of the fruit, and pray that he will help you do it even better.

. . . .

Bible in a year: Ezekiel 36,37; Psalms 126–128

Clean up

PREPARE

'My heart says of you, "Seek his face!" Your face, LORD, I will seek' (Psalm 27:8).

READ

Luke 11:37–54

EXPLORE

Lunch with a Pharisee – lovely! A perfect mission opportunity for Jesus, or so you'd think! But it doesn't turn out that way. Instead, it all kicks off when Jesus doesn't wash his hands (v 38) – a religious ritual for supposedly getting rid of any stains guests might have picked up from the sinful world outside. And right there is the problem. The Pharisees are all about how things look on the outside, no matter how rotten things are inside.

Now of course we're not Pharisees or law teachers opposing Jesus – we're his followers – but we need to be sure there's no hint of what Jesus accuses them of *in us*. If it's wrong for them, it's got to be wrong for us. Let's be prayerful and careful about this. The sense of what Jesus says is devastating. For instance, it's like:

- cups and dishes (vs 39–41) that look nice and clean on the outside but are filthy inside where it really matters;
- measuring out pinches of herbs (v 42) while you ignore the weight of the world's injustices;
- everyone looking admiringly your way, except God (v 43);
- thinking you're walking the way of life, when actually you're treading the pathway to death (v 44) and taking plenty of others with you.

God looks down from heaven on all mankind to see if there are any who understand, any who seek God.

Psalm 53:2

RESPOND

Discipleship often involves self-examination, though we often forget. Pray about any issues raised today for you, or any from the rest of this series of readings.

Bible in a year: Ezekiel 38,39; 2 Peter 3

Sunday 20 November
Psalm 72

The King and I

PREPARE
Imagine entering the throne room of a king. What preparation, if any, would help you make sure you're ready to meet him? But God the King wants us just to come as we are, but with love and respect. Ready?

READ
Psalm 72

EXPLORE
You won't have got far through this song before you realised there's something strange about it. It seems to be a prayer for the ruler of Israel, who's a descendant of King David, but then it uses phrases such as 'May he endure as long as the sun…' (v 5). Well, none of David's descendants lived and reigned *that* long, did they? Except one, of course: the Lord Jesus himself (Matthew 1:6–16; Luke 1:32,33). The song is about Solomon or his son, but it also stretches to be about Jesus.

Scattered through the song are pointers to what the role of the king's followers should be. Scanning the verses again, how much can you see in them about this, if we're to work with him in what he's doing?

One thing I notice for Jesus' followers, from verse 17b, is that we are to join God in his mission, the same mission he wanted Abram and Sarai to join in with back in Genesis 12:1–3: 'blessing' everyone on earth by helping them to know God through Jesus.

Praise be to his glorious name for ever; may the whole earth be filled with his glory. Amen and Amen.

Psalm 72:19

RESPOND
Pray for yourself in your own community, that you'll find ways of connecting with those who don't yet know Jesus the King and pointing them to him.

Bible in a year: Ezekiel 40,41; 1 John 1

Scripture Union

By purchasing *Daily Bread*, you are helping to support Scripture Union's mission with children and young people. Thank you!

Subscribe to our free supporter and prayer magazine at su.org.uk/ connectingyou

Living life God's way

About the writer
Louisa King

Louisa King lives in Sheffield with her young family. She loves being part of her church family, and likes meeting people or journaling and reading in cafes.

Our readings over the next week or so are part of a range of teachings that Jesus gave his disciples and various crowds. They are making their way towards Jerusalem, where Jesus would ultimately be crucified and rise again.

And they are challenging readings! In them, Jesus frequently juxtaposes a life of repentance and following God versus a life without God. His teaching was sometimes so popular that people trampled over each other (12:1)! But he wasn't always so popular. So, we will be asked to consider our love for and commitment to God in a world that doesn't generally seek to follow him. We will meet people who are listening to Jesus (as well as some who are determinedly not); we will meet those living wise and faithful lives (and those who are not). So, let's pray that we listen to Jesus carefully and with wisdom as we study his Word over the coming days.

One of my favourite readings in this collection is in Luke 13:10–13 where Jesus sees a disabled woman and beckons her to come to him, and he heals her. As we begin these readings, let us ask God to give us eyes to see how he loves us and is calling us to come to him and follow him, even when we might feel unworthy. We will also read in Luke 12:28–30 that God will clothe us and give us all we need, so we don't need to worry. We have a God who cares for us and for where we're at. May that encourage you today.

Fear God!

PREPARE
'He restores my soul. He leads me in paths of righteousness for his name's sake' (Psalm 23:3, ESV). Consider how you feel today. Rest a moment before you read God's Word.

. . . .

READ
Luke 12:1–12

EXPLORE
In chapter 11, Jesus has been telling his disciples to be on their guard against people (eg the Pharisees) who might try to dissuade them from following him. He continues this theme in verse 1. Can you think of things which might distract or dissuade you from following Jesus today?

There will come a time 'before the angels of God' (vs 8,9), when Jesus, the Son of Man, will either acknowledge us as his followers... or reject us. At this point, God will bring light to things which are currently in darkness (vs 2,3). Jesus alone is the way to life after death (vs 5,8). So, Jesus tells us to fear God rather than other people, for God is the One who:

- forgives us (v 10);
- loves and cares for us (vs 6,7);
- gives us words to say when we are under pressure (v 12).

Verse 10 might cause some to worry that we have spoken against the Holy Spirit. But Jesus is referring to those who persistently reject his message. Those who tend towards worrying about this have no need to fear, for their hearts are already open towards God.

'... fear him who, after your body has been killed, has authority to throw you into hell. Yes, I tell you, fear him.'
Luke 12:5

RESPOND
Turn to the distractions you considered earlier. Are there things you need to repent for? Ask the Holy Spirit to fill your heart with God's love and with openness to follow him.

. . . .

Bible in a year: Ezekiel 42,43; 1 John 2

Tuesday 22 November
Luke 12:13–21

Be on your guard!

PREPARE

'For from him and through him and for him are all things. To him be the glory for ever! Amen' (Romans 11:36). Pause and reflect on how everything comes from God and is for him and his glory.

READ
Luke 12:13–21

EXPLORE

I have read this story many times with my children as it appears with comical pictures in their children's Bible! And it does feel a bit silly, doesn't it? A man who already has more than enough keeps working hard for more things he doesn't need, which in the end he doesn't get to enjoy properly because he dies before he can 'take life easy' and enjoy them (vs 16–20).

Notice how much the man is focused on himself: there are lots of '*I* will do this…' and '*my* crops', '*my* barns' and '*my* grain' (vs 17,18). His life is centred on himself, not God – and God says to him, 'You fool!' (v 20).

Could this be us too? It's certainly not easy to step outside the materialistic world in which we live, but Jesus reminds us of our eternal destiny, where our earthly possessions simply will not matter or be significant. Let us seek God rather than the distractions and arguments about our possessions (v 13).

'Watch out! Be on your guard against all kinds of greed; life does not consist in an abundance of possessions.'
Luke 12:15

RESPOND
Pray through what it might mean for you to shift your attention from your possessions to being 'rich towards God' (v 21). Pray for your church community, that it would also have this attitude.

Bible in a year: Ezekiel 44,45; Psalms 129–131

Do not be anxious!

PREPARE

If you can, head outside or to a window, and spend some time observing God's creation (whatever that might be where you are!), and thank God for all he has created and sustains.

•••

READ
Luke 12:22–34

EXPLORE

We live in an anxious world, full of unknowns and things over which we have no control, and sometimes, a command not to be anxious (v 22) can feel overwhelmingly unattainable.

But Jesus was not speaking from an ivory tower. After all, he spent his life talking to different people with various worries, concerns and ailments. In this passage, he recognises we might worry about food, drink and clothes (vs 23,29) or our lifespan (v 25). His tone is not chastising. In fact, he points us to a tender God who feeds birds (v 24) and delights in simple things like grass and flowers (vs 27,28).

Our Father is a God who loves and values us (v 24) and gives us what we need (v 30). So instead of being anxious, we are to aim to seek God and to care for others (vs 31–34). As Paul prayed for his brothers and sisters in Christ, 'May the God of hope fill you with all joy and peace as you trust in him, so that you may overflow with hope by the power of the Holy Spirit' (Romans 15:13).

> Then Jesus said to his disciples: 'Therefore I tell you, do not worry about your life, what you will eat; or about your body, what will you wear.'
> **Luke 12:22**

RESPOND

Whatever anxieties you are facing, pray that the Holy Spirit will fill you with peace and hope in God's love, as you trust in his care and provision today.

•••

Bible in a year: Ezekiel 46,47; 1 John 3

Thursday 24 November
Luke 12:35–48

Be ready!

PREPARE
What are you waiting for or looking forward to? Pray about it!

. . . .

READ
Luke 12:35–48

EXPLORE
Are you ready for the Lord's return? Jesus gives us various images in today's passage to help us think about this.

The first (vs 36–38) is about servants waiting for their master to come home from a wedding banquet. Will they be awake and ready to serve him when he arrives – however unexpectedly (v 40)? A second image (vs 39,40) focuses on the owner of the house. It gets to the crux of the matter. Like a houseowner who does not know when his house will be broken into, we *don't know* when Jesus (the 'Son of Man') will return. Another image (vs 42–46) is about two different kinds of servant: one is faithful and wise; the other cruel and profligate. So, how can we be faithful and trustworthy servants in our living today?

We must be ready – and point others to being ready too, for there will be punishment for those who do not act according to God's will (vs 46–48). What does this being ready look like? Jesus applauds the manager in verses 42 and 43, who operates his life with wise faithfulness. While we can't be physically awake 24/7 – even Jesus slept (Luke 8:23,24) – we can stay alert in our relationship with the Lord (vs 35,36).

'You also must be ready, because the Son of Man will come at an hour when you do not expect him.'
Luke 12:40

RESPOND
Sing or listen to the song 'Speak, O Lord' (Stuart Townend, Keith Getty)* and think about what living with wisdom and faithfulness might look like for you.

*There are several versions on YouTube

. . . .

Bible in a year: Ezekiel 48; 1 John 4

Expect division!

PREPARE
Think about the stories in the news headlines today. Some will undoubtedly speak of division and discord. Then turn your eyes to the God who made the world and is above it all.

. . . .

READ
Luke 12:49–59

EXPLORE
We live in a world that is divided, often unbearably so, and riven with tension, war and conflict – with examples like those which Jesus speaks of in verses 52 and 53. And it might surprise us, but Jesus' response is not necessarily one of peace (vs 49–51).

Instead, his words point us to a world that is divided between those who follow God and those who don't. Jesus has come to save people and connect them with God (the 'baptism' referred to in verse 50 probably refers to his own suffering and death).

So, the question for us is: do we follow Jesus as our Saviour (see Romans 3:23–25) in spite of how others judge us? And what does that look like in our divided world? In verses 54,55 and verses 57–59, Jesus gives two examples of people operating with wisdom in their daily interactions. So, too, may we understand Jesus' words here and know what he is saying to us (v 56). How should we be interpreting our own times?

'Hypocrites! You know how to interpret the appearance of the earth and the sky. How is it that you don't know how to interpret this present time?'
Luke 12:56

RESPOND
Ours is not a world which routinely follows God, and many have not turned to Jesus. Consider how you might share your story of faith in Jesus with someone who doesn't know him (see https://twowaystolive.com as an example).

Bible in a year: Daniel 1–3; Psalms 132–134

Saturday 26 November
Luke 13:1–9

Turn to God!

PREPARE
Pray through these verses: 'Have mercy on me, O God, according to your unfailing love; according to your great compassion blot out my transgressions. Wash away all my iniquity and cleanse me from my sin.' (Psalm 51:1,2).

....

READ
Luke 13:1–9

PREPARE
The main focus of this passage is set out in verses 3 and 5: we must repent and turn to God.

Consider God as a master gardener, as he is in other parts of the Bible (eg John 15:1–17): in verses 6–9, he is tending to his vineyard. He agrees to give his fig tree another year to see if it responds to some additional love and care – and if it doesn't, it will be cut down.

God's world is like the fig tree. Will it respond and grow according to God's word and direction, or will it perish?

Jesus is clear in verses 1–5: people don't perish or experience particularly awful situations because they are worse than other people (see also John 9:2,3); there are no categories of sinners – we are all sinful and need God. And God is gracious, giving his fig tree an extra year to respond to his attentions (vs 8,9). How will we respond to his reaching out to us?

'... unless you repent, you too will all perish.'
Luke 13:5

RESPOND
Spend some time in prayer and worship. 'See to it that you do not refuse him who speaks... let us be thankful, and so worship God acceptably with reverence and awe' (Hebrews 12:25,28).

....

Bible in a year: Daniel 4,5; 1 John 5

The Lord is our refuge!

PREPARE

Jesus says, 'Come to me, all you who are weary and burdened, and I will give you rest' (Matthew 11:28). Come to Christ today and ask him for rest.

READ

Psalm 73

EXPLORE

In our readings in Luke, Jesus has been teaching about the different paths one could take in life – and this psalm follows a similar theme. It's a 'wisdom' psalm, with the psalmist exploring some of the themes from his life, from which we can also learn.

The psalmist sets out the way of 'the arrogant' and 'the wicked' in verses 3–12, a path which can feel attractive to us – who wouldn't want to avoid being 'plagued by human ills', (v 5)? Do you sometimes feel conflicted between living God's way and living in the way of the world? Sometimes, the apparently carefree lives of the wicked don't seem fair (v 12)! But in the end, the wicked will perish (vs 18–20,27) – and it will be God's doing (v 18).

Meanwhile, like the psalmist, we can feel weary (v 16) – Jesus did too! – and even bitter (v 21). But verses 23–28 are a marvellous expression of what it means to have faith. Unlike the psalmist, we *know* that Jesus has conquered over all – and we can be near God because of all he achieved for us on the cross (v 28). 'Surely God is good' (v 1).

> But as for me, it is good to be near God. I have made the Sovereign LORD my refuge; I will tell of all your deeds.

Psalm 73:28

RESPOND

Read through Psalm 49 – another wisdom psalm – and pray for God to give you wisdom to live in today's world.

Bible in a year: Daniel 6,7; 2 John

Monday 28 November

Luke 13:10–17

Seen by Jesus!

PREPARE

You may well be reading this on a Monday morning. Come to Jesus today and bring your week ahead to him. Where do you need his help and healing?

· ·

READ

Luke 13:10–17

EXPLORE

This is a wonderful story to lead on from some of the passages last week, which spoke fiercely of the reality of our divided world. An essential part of the good news of Jesus is that he brings healing and liberation! (And this is something we should celebrate, not criticise or be nit-picky about – see vs 14–16.)

Imagine yourself as the woman in this passage: disabled for many years; in pain; unable to stand up straight to see and respond to the world around her – and, therefore, impoverished and a bit of an outcast – more tied up than some donkeys (vs 15,16). And Jesus sees her, touches her and heals her (v 13).

It is a remarkable thing that Jesus, a healthy man – in what was likely to be a crowded synagogue – *saw* this woman. And he didn't just see her; he also healed her. The only thing appropriate for us is to rejoice, to thank and praise God – as the woman and the people watching did (vs 13,17) – and to keep turning to him for help and healing.

> ... his opponents were humiliated, but the people were delighted with all the wonderful things he was doing.
>
> **Luke 13:17**

RESPOND

Sing or listen to the hymn, 'And Can It Be':*
'Long my imprisoned spirit lay, / ... / Thine eye diffused a quick'ning ray – / ... / My chains fell off, my heart was free, / I rose, went forth, and followed thee.'

*'And Can It Be', Charles Wesley, 1738.

· ·

Bible in a year: Daniel 8,9; 3 John

Enter God's kingdom!

PREPARE
Think about your life and your church family. Where can you see evidence of God at work? Praise God for this.

....

READ
Luke 13:18–30

EXPLORE
You will probably notice as you read these verses that some themes in this passage resemble those we have looked at over the past few days. Who is going to be in the kingdom of God? We know that not all will be saved in our divided world (vs 25–28); we also know that some will be saved and will experience God's healing and blessing (v 29).

As well as this, our passage today talks about what God's kingdom is like. And the answer? It's everywhere! It's like a mustard seed that grows into a healthy, growing tree (v 19), and yeast that spreads through a ball of dough (v 21). People will come from east and west and north and south (v 29) – so God's kingdom spreads and flows – including some you might not expect.

Verse 30 should make us pause for thought. Clearly, God's kingdom does not necessarily share the same values as our world – a bit like our story yesterday when Jesus saw an unseen woman and healed her. So, let's be on the lookout for God at work in unseen, unexpected ways – and ask him for the faith to see him at work.

> 'People will come from east and west and north and south, and will take their places at the feast in the kingdom of God.'
>
> **Luke 13:29**

RESPOND
Pray the Lord's Prayer, and ask for God's kingdom to come on earth today – in your life, in your church family and in the world.

....

Bible in a year: Daniel 10–12; Psalms 135,136

Wednesday 30 November

Luke 13:31–35

Jesus is Lord!

PREPARE

'Dear Lord Jesus, thank you that you are King over all, and you love me so much that you died for me and rose again.'

READ

Luke 13:31–35

EXPLORE

Jesus has been acting and teaching in a controversial way, and clearly this has got the attention of the local authorities (v 31). But Jesus is not surprised by this; the Bible is full of stories of God's prophets not being welcomed by those around them.

Jerusalem is the centre for Jesus' attention (and God's story of his people): Jesus knows that he will die there and has been journeying towards it (v 33; Luke 9:44). God has long loved and protected his people (see Deuteronomy 32:10–12; Psalms 17:8; 36:7) – but as we have seen in earlier passages, not all will respond to Jesus' message of salvation, and this leads Jesus to lament (vs 34,35). What things are stirring your heart to lament about today?

Jesus' message about Jerusalem and the people of Israel is another example of God's kingdom not being quite what we would expect. We know that those who aren't of the biological family of Israel will also be invited into God's kingdom if they turn to Jesus (see Galatians 3:26–29). There is much to praise God for.

'Blessed is he who comes in the name of the Lord.'

Luke 13:35

RESPOND

Luke 13:35 repeats words from Psalm 118:26, which some have interpreted as a prophecy about the coming of Jesus. Read Psalm 118 through now, reflecting on its words to prompt your prayers for today.

Bible in a year: Hosea 1,2; Jude

Have it your way

About the writer
Jo Swinney

Jo Swinney is Director of Church Communications at CPO, a speaker and an author, most recently of *Home: the quest to belong* (Hodder & Stoughton). She has an MA in theology from Regent College, Vancouver, and lives in Surbiton with her husband and their two daughters.

I can't sugar-coat it: these chapters at the end of Jeremiah are brutal. We are going to be reading our way through a dire period of Israel's history, watching them make decision after terrible decision and reaping the seeds they have chosen to sow. Jeremiah faithfully delivers God's warnings – getting himself into a whole lot of trouble as a result – but Israel and her leaders are not listening. What unfolds is therefore on their heads.

That may be logical, but it is still unsettling and upsetting to encounter the outworking of God's anger on this stiff-necked nation of his: slow starvation under siege; large-scale slaughter; the desecration of their Temple; exile from the Promised Land.

It is OK to acknowledge our discomfort. We can come to God with our questions, our fears, our dismay at the harshness and vitriol of these words his prophet says are his. He has given us his Holy Spirit to reveal him to us; he sent his Son to walk among us. He will help us wrestle through these troubling episodes in salvation history.

In all his dealings with us, God gives us freedom. It is this freedom which enables genuine relationship between the divine and us, who are made in his image. God, through Jeremiah, urged his people to repent and be his again. And in the end, he let them have it their way. The same choice is ours today.

(Im)possible standards

PREPARE
Come confidently but humbly before the throne of our holy God today.

. . . .

READ
Jeremiah 35:1–19

EXPLORE
Your church leader has an affair with a married congregant. A Christian business owner is convicted of tax fraud. A well-known Christian author is exposed as a plagiarist. You might be forgiven for thinking there is no one without feet of clay, not a single, genuinely godly person on this planet. And after all, we are human. How could we ever meet God's standards for holy living?

Jeremiah had moments of profound discouragement and dismay living and ministering in a largely faithless, idolatrous, corrupt society as he did. But here he is meeting a group of people who break the mould. The Rekabite family – every member in every generation since their ancestor Jehonadab gave the commands – have been obedient to a set of harsh restrictions, from an alcohol ban through to having to live in tents instead of houses. When Jeremiah offers them wine, they risk offence or worse and turn it down. They are obedient in ways large and small, individual and corporate, public and private. 'Learn a lesson!' God says (v13). It can be done.

'This is what the LORD Almighty, the God of Israel, says: go and tell the people of Judah and those living in Jerusalem, "Will you not learn a lesson and obey my words?" declares the LORD.'
Jeremiah 35:13

RESPOND
We are in a race, and our goal is to cross the finish line (Hebrews 12:1). Being distracted by those who have fallen will break our stride and slow us down. Identify the Rekabites in your life – they do exist – and be inspired by them.

. . . .

Bible in a year: Hosea 3–6; Revelation 1

Rulers behaving badly

PREPARE
'Thank you for your Word, Lord, a lamp to my feet and a light for my path. Amen' (based on Psalm 119:105).

READ
Jeremiah 36:1–32

EXPLORE

At my daughter's school, there is assigned seating for every class. In her philosophy, ethics and theology class (religious education has had a rebrand apparently!), she sits next to a boy called Harry, who mutters continually under his breath, 'Load of rubbish. No such thing as God. What a waste of time.' Charis is shocked by his disrespect for beliefs other people hold dear. But I'm not shocked. There have always been people who despise and ridicule God and his followers.

Today's reading is a good example. On a day of fasting before the Lord, where people gathered from Jerusalem and other towns in Judah, the king and his officials were hunkered down cosily by the fire in the winter apartment (v 22). That is noteworthily rude, but worse is to come. On hearing the words of the Lord himself, given to Jeremiah, dictated to Baruch the scribe, he burns the scroll piece by piece (v 23).

In the words of Taylor Swift, 'haters gonna hate'.* But God won't be mocked, and we reap what we sow (Galatians 6:7). This scroll was a lifeline, an invitation to turn from the way of death and choose life. Burning it was a bad decision.

'Perhaps when the people of Judah hear about every disaster I plan to inflict on them, they will each turn from their wicked ways; then I will forgive their wickedness and their sin.'

Jeremiah 36:3

RESPOND
We may not brazenly rip out Bible pages, but can we truthfully say we treat it *all* with due reverence? Here is an opportunity to turn and be forgiven.

*'Shake It Off', Taylor Swift, © 2014, Big Machine Records.

Bible in a year: Hosea 7,8; Psalms 137,138

Saturday 3 December

Jeremiah 37:1–21

Not just a friend in need

PREPARE

'Father God, help me to live always mindful of your presence, worshipping in spirit and truth every moment of the day. Amen.'

....

READ

Jeremiah 37:1–21

EXPLORE

There's a new king on the throne, Zedekiah, puppet of the Babylonians (v 1). There may be a new leader, but the text tells us baldly: nothing has changed. No one 'paid any attention to the words the LORD had spoken...' (v 2).

King Zedekiah is slightly different to his predecessor though. In crunch moments, he asks for prayer (v 3) and wants to hear what God might have said lately to Jeremiah (v 17).

There is a profoundly human instinct to pray *in extremis*, or at least to ask someone else to pray. I've been contacted in the middle of the night by an atheist friend in labour, grabbed at the school gate by a teacher waiting for a biopsy result, texted out of the blue by a previous colleague having a mental health crisis, all saying a variation of 'Please pray for me!' As the saying goes, there are no atheists in foxholes.

God's ears are not deaf to the cries of the desperate who, until now, had paid him no mind at all. He welcomed the criminal on the cross beside him into paradise without a second's hesitation after all (Luke 23:42–43). But we have a God who calls us friend (John 15:15), and only turning to him when we are desperate is not a great way to treat a friend.

'Please pray to the LORD our God for us.'

Jeremiah 37:3

RESPOND

Set aside your needs, and seek the Lord now, with no agenda.

....

Bible in a year: Hosea 9,10; Revelation 2

Everlasting

PREPARE
Are you tired? Are you discouraged? Come to the God who gives rest to the weary and increases the power of the weak and be restored.

READ
Psalm 74

EXPLORE
A couple recently returned from living in Greece have joined our church. 'Thessaloniki, Philippi, the Acropolis – the church there is non-existent,' they said sadly. 'To think what it was and now no worshipping community at all.' As with the Temple in Jerusalem, over and over again, sanctuaries in these key New Testament places are in ruins. How could you have let this happen? How long will the enemy mock you, God (v 10)?

In some places in the world – often where there is harshest opposition – the church is flourishing spiritually and numerically. But in many others, we Christians are an increasingly unpopular and tiny minority. Does this mean God has lost his grip? Is he losing the cosmic battle for the salvation of the world? No! When the psalmist says the day and night, summer and winter are his, he's saying, 'All time is God's.' When he says God opens springs and dries rivers, he's

saying the life and death of everything is in God's hands (vs 15–17). Battles may be lost, but the war is won. Long live the King, on the throne for ever and ever.

But God is my King from long ago; he brings salvation on the earth.

Psalm 74:12

RESPOND
'Oh Lord, haunts of violence *still* fill the dark places of the land (v 20). May your kingdom come. May it come in me and through me. Come, Lord Jesus. Amen.'

Bible in a year: Hosea 11,12; Revelation 3

Monday 5 December
Jeremiah 38:1–28

Passive power

PREPARE

'Lord, help me step up into the responsibilities I have today. Bless the work of my hands and others through me. Amen.'

· ·

READ
Jeremiah 38:1–28

EXPLORE

The idea of power is so seductive some notable leaders have been driven to do great evil in its pursuit – think Joseph Stalin, Adolph Hitler, Mao Zedong, Pol Pot. And then there is King Zedekiah. He has the throne and yet he seems to want none of the responsibility it confers: 'the king can do nothing' apparently (v 5). He washes his hands of Jeremiah much as Pilate sought to do of Jesus (Matthew 27:24). Later, he sits quietly in the knowledge that by surrendering to Babylon he could save himself, Jerusalem and its inhabitants. His refusals to make decisions were, of course, decisions.

It is not just kings who have power. Each of us does, whether you lead an organisation, a church small group or a party-planning committee; whether you are a parent, a member of a friendship group or a sports team; whether you are a judge or just have the right to vote.

And every day we have the choice how to exercise dominion over our areas of influence. We can lead in line with God's rule of his kingdom or according to the 'pattern of this world' (Romans 12:2). There is no third option.

> 'He is in your hands,' King Zedekiah answered. 'The king can do nothing to oppose you.'
>
> **Jeremiah 38:5**

RESPOND

Consider the places and situations where you have influence. How can you use your power, however limited, to bring God's kingdom?

· ·

Bible in a year: Hosea 13,14; Revelation 4

Relational logic

PREPARE
Take a few minutes to sit in God's company, both speaking and listening.

• •

READ
Jeremiah 39:1–18

EXPLORE
The proof of the pudding is in the eating, so they say. Jeremiah's prophetic credentials are no longer in doubt once the gruesome 18-month siege of Jerusalem comes to its fiery, bloody end. He has faithfully conveyed God's warnings and repeated request that Israel turns from its idols and corrupt ways, and in the light of their failure to respond, the consequence plays out as it was predicted. The narrative recounts apocalyptic scenes of devastation, and we wonder: What does this say about God? How can he both be loving and allow such horror to unfold?

This is one of the great questions, and it can't be dealt with in a few trite sentences. But the answer is not that the evidence forces us to conclude God is not loving, in which case who would want anything to do with him? For today, let's just concentrate on Ebed-Melek, the African we met yesterday, spearheading Jeremiah's rescue from the cistern (38:7–13). Why did God save his life? Not because he saved Jeremiah's, but because he trusted the Lord (vs 15–18). God is a person, not a formula. The logic is relational and the answer lies in his character.

'I will save you; you will not fall by the sword but will escape with your life, because you trust in me, declares the LORD.'
Jeremiah 39:18

RESPOND
'Lord God, I don't understand your ways. How could I? You are God and I am not. But I do trust you. Please increase my trust. Amen.'

• •

Bible in a year: Joel 1,2; Psalm 139

Wednesday 7 December

Jeremiah 40:1 – 41:15

Yet I will hope

PREPARE

A dashed hope or vanishing dream can easily make us bitter. Ask the Holy Spirit to bring you peace and comfort as you deal with disappointments large and small.

READ

Jeremiah 40:1 – 41:15

EXPLORE

This is a profoundly painful and messy chapter for the people of God, not least because it begins so optimistically. Gedaliah, appointed to govern Judah by the Babylonians, appears to be a good man and a wise leader (v 5). He is able to rally the remnant, refocus them on the harvest (vs 7–10), and with echoes of Jeremiah's letter to the exiles in chapter 29, to encourage them to live peaceably under the new regime. It could have all turned out so well.

You have read what happened, so you know how it went down (40:13 – 41:3). Perhaps it reminded you of times the government has passed policies that harmed the most vulnerable in our society, or of watching someone you love get sicker and sicker and then die of cancer, or of being made redundant and then losing your house.

It often seems that God allows the worst to come about. If we make it our belief that he is a loving, powerful and good God, contingent on life coming up rosy, our faith is going to hit the rocks sooner than later. With Job, we must find a way to say, 'Though he slay me, yet will I hope in him' (Job 13:15).

> Ishmael … got up and struck down Gedaliah … with the sword, killing the one whom the king of Babylon had appointed as governor over the land.
>
> **Jeremiah 41:2**

RESPOND

'But now, Lord, what do I look for? My hope is in you' (Psalm 39:7).

Bible in a year: Joel 3; Revelation 5

Go with God

PREPARE
'Speak, Lord. I am listening.'

....

READ
Jeremiah 41:16 – 43:13

EXPLORE
How do you approach a big decision? Some go with their head, some with their heart. This bedraggled band of refugees say they want to go with God: 'Pray that the LORD your God will tell us where we should go and what we should do' (42:3). Before we dismiss them for cheap lip service, let's remember they had lived through two horrific years of invasion, siege, the death or exile of most of their compatriots, internal displacement, civil war and the ongoing threat of the Babylonians from the north. And yet they were willing to pause on the road for ten whole days while they waited for God's direction (42:7).

When it came, it wasn't what they wanted to hear. And so, the story takes an acutely ironic turn. The direct ancestors of those God had dramatically rescued from 400 years of slavery in Egypt return willingly to their bondage (43:7).

It is understandable to fear pain, hunger and loss and to do what we can to avoid those things. But throughout the Bible, over and over again, God says, 'Fear not. I am with you' (eg Isaiah 41:10). The worst that can happen to us is separation from God. Making our decisions on that basis is the way of wisdom.

'Do not be afraid of the king of Babylon, whom you now fear. Do not be afraid of him, declares the LORD, for I am with you and will save you and deliver you from his hands.'
Jeremiah 42:11

RESPOND
'Lord, help me trust you with all my heart, not leaning on my own understanding. Make my paths straight, I pray. Amen.'

....

Bible in a year: Amos 1,2; Revelation 6

Friday 9 December

Jeremiah 44:1 – 45:5

Not what we deserve

PREPARE

'Humble yourselves before the Lord, and he will lift you up' (James 4:10).

. . . .

READ

Jeremiah 44:1 – 45:5

EXPLORE

Back in Egypt, our motley crew from Judea seem keen to blend in and are soon committing eye-wateringly brazen idolatry (v 8). Those awful people, not listening to God, are pouring out offerings to the Queen of Heaven and making cakes impressed with her image (44:19)! However terrible their behaviour, though, to our modern sensibilities the subsequent judgement is almost equally abhorrent. We aren't comfortable with the idea of God punishing anyone at all, let alone by sword, famine and plague (44:13).

After I read today's passage, I messaged my friend: 'God says, "I will bring disaster on all people" (45:5). Help! How do I find a devotional application for that?' A couple of minutes later he replied, 'Disaster is what we deserve, isn't it? A good reminder of how much patience and mercy God has with us.'

When we encounter the wrath of God in scripture, we have to remember his anger is righteous, justified and fully deserved ('For the wages of sin is death', Romans 6:23). If we are shocked, it should be because he holds back so long and has never ceased to show mercy.

> 'Again and again I sent my servants the prophets, who said, "Do not do this detestable thing that I hate!"'
> **Jeremiah 44:4**

RESPOND

'Father God, you do not treat us as our sins deserve ... so great is your love for those who fear you; as far as the east is from the west, so far have you removed our transgressions from us' (based on Psalm 103:10–12).

. . . .

Bible in a year: Amos 3,4; Psalms 140,141

Some things never change

PREPARE
Come to the Rock of Ages, whose love is everlasting and whose mercies never change.

··

READ
Jeremiah 46:1 – 47:7

EXPLORE
Let's assess the situation for God's chosen people at this juncture in history. They have fallen a long way from the heights of life under David's kingship, with a large, growing and united kingdom. Now the best of them have been killed or taken into Babylonian exile, the remnant have fled to Egypt, and Jerusalem lies in ruins (44:1–6). What is going on? Has God changed sides?

If we are to have any understanding of God's relationship with Israel at this point, we need to get inside the meaning of 'covenant' because this underpins all their dealings with each other. As we read, there are three aspects of God's covenant with Israel we need to remember. First, a covenant is relational, not legal in nature; God's dealings with his people are personal, not procedural (v 27). Secondly, each party in the covenant makes promises and understands that breaking them entails consequences (vs 28b; 44:1–6). Israel had consistently broken their side of the covenant, hence they are experiencing God's judgement. Thirdly, God always goes above and beyond his obligations, even to the establishment of a new covenant made in his blood (Luke 22:20). Things may seem hopeless, but God is still with Israel (vs 27,28). There is no need to fear.

'Do not be afraid, Jacob my servant, for I am with you,' declares the LORD.
Jeremiah 46:28

RESPOND
In the midst of political, environmental and societal upheaval we can feel small and vulnerable. Ask the Lord to replace your fear with peace and the certainty of his presence with you.

··

Bible in a year: Amos 5,6; Revelation 7

Sunday 11 December
Psalm 75

Dangerous pride

PREPARE
Spend a few minutes praising God and considering his character and works.

....

READ
Psalm 75

EXPLORE
This psalm presents two extremes, with God in the centre seeing and responding to each as they deserve. It is a helpful picture, though worth remembering there aren't clear-cut goodies and baddies in real life. Most of us are a big mix of both, dependent on God's grace in everything.

Here, though, we have an either/or. There are 'the arrogant' (v 4). These people boast and flaunt their 'horns' – a symbol of strength, audaciously picking a fight with heaven itself! The psalmist is scathing, pointing out that no one can exalt themselves (v 6). We could walk out of our houses right now and declare to the street that we are now in charge of the universe, but we'd be laughed at (or taken away for psychiatric evaluation).

On the other hand, we have the righteous, who understand their place. They praise God and know he has all the power, and that they have none if he hasn't given it (v 7). It is these people God lifts up, granting them honour and strength.

Pride is a perennial temptation. It distorts our perspective, enlarging us and minimising God, and it has devastating consequences. Thankfully, we have a loving father willing to discipline us for our own good, to forgive us and to continue working on our characters.

'When the earth and all its people quake, it is I who hold its pillars firm.'
Psalm 75:3

RESPOND
We are all susceptible to pride. Come before God in repentance now, and ask him to humble you.

....

Bible in a year: Amos 7,8; Revelation 8

Shared anguish

PREPARE
As Jesus instructed, pray for those who persecute you today (Matthew 5:44).

. . . .

READ
Jeremiah 48:1–25

EXPLORE
This is a painful oracle. The kingdom of Moab, though historically an enemy, had had close ties with Israel-Judah for hundreds of years (Genesis 19:30–38). King David's ancestor Ruth was a Moabite (Ruth 1:22), and his parents had sought refuge there (1 Samuel 22:3–5). Visible to Judah over the rift valley, they had close familiarity with each other. Having formed an ill-fated alliance against Babylon (27:3), both experienced the same devastation: slaughter for most; exile for the rest (v 7).

While geographically close, the kingdom of Moab was far from its neighbour in that they had their own god, Chemosh (vs 7,13). Trusting Chemosh and themselves, they had become complacent and eventually as rank and bitter as undecanted wine (v 11).

The people of Israel, though brought as low, had the lifeline of God's covenantal love and mercy. They might have been tempted, if not to gloat, to feel smug and a little superior. Maybe you recognise that tendency – I do. But the imperative here is to mourn: to grieve the terrible suffering of others, regardless of its cause. There is nothing to celebrate here.

'Mourn for her, all who live around her, all who know her fame; say, "How broken is the mighty sceptre, how broken the glorious staff!"'
Jeremiah 48:17

RESPOND
'Lord, give me a soft heart towards the sufferings of others, even if they seem to deserve it or have brought it on themselves. By your Holy Spirit, empower me to pray for my enemies. Amen.'

. . . .

Bible in a year: Amos 9; Revelation 9

Tuesday 13 December

Jeremiah 48:26–47

Divine grief

PREPARE

Take your concerns and struggles to your loving heavenly Father.

• •

READ

Jeremiah 48:26–47

EXPLORE

What is God like? There are many places we can go in search of answers to that all-important question. In the 500s BC, God's actions, the prophets, and their interpretation of events gave foundational insight: insight which we gain from too.

So, what can we glean from today's passage? Moab lies desolate, food production has stopped, the whole land echoes with the sound of weeping, and all this at God's instigation: 'I have stopped the flow of wine' (v 33); 'I will put an end to those who make offerings' (v 35); 'I have broken Moab...' (v 38). From this, we see God is holy and is angered by sin and especially idolatry. God is powerful and fearful. But there are other qualities shown here too, which prevent us mischaracterising him as cruel, sadistic or cold.

Ezekiel tells us God gets no pleasure from the death of the wicked (Ezekiel 18:23), but here it goes much further than neutrality – the enactment of his righteous judgement causes him profound pain: 'I wail ... I cry out ... I moan ... I weep for you ... my heart laments ...' (vs 31,32,36).

In Jesus, God has revealed to us his true nature, the fullness of himself in human form. And his crucifixion is the ultimate picture of God's own suffering in the judgement of our sin (Isaiah 53:4–6).

'I weep for you...'

Jeremiah 48:32

RESPOND

Thank God that you have peace with him through the blood of Jesus, shed on the cross (Colossians 1:20).

• •

Bible in a year: Obadiah; Psalms 142,143

By the same measure

PREPARE
'Your kingdom come, your will be done, on earth as it is in heaven. Amen.'

. . . .

READ
Jeremiah 49:1–39

EXPLORE
When humans set up societies or systems in direct opposition to God, things go very badly wrong. God's way is not arbitrary, illogical or set up to benefit only him: in his kingdom everything and everyone flourishes. Look out for glimpses of this in these verses (vs 6,39) and as we wait in hope of eternal life in its fullness.

In Jeremiah's time, life for most was basic, bloody and brutal. Medicine was primitive, food production fragile and national boundaries in constant flux. As a result, most societies were violent, warmongering and dependent on superstition and false gods.

The Mosaic Law shone a path towards a communal life based on love, altruism and mutual care and respect which, if the people of Israel had embraced it, would have set them entirely apart from their neighbours. We've seen how far they fell and the ensuing consequences.

The five prophecies in chapter 49 concern kingdoms surrounding Israel and Judah. God is the God of the whole world, and it isn't just his chosen people who fall under judgement. Neither is his offer of restitution and redemption (vs 6,39) limited. In fact, Acts 2:9 tells us people from Elam were among those to hear the apostles preach on the day of Pentecost. Their downfall is dreadful but not the end of the story.

'Yet I will restore the fortunes of Elam in days to come,' declares the LORD.

Jeremiah 49:39

> ## RESPOND
> How can you bring God's ways to bear in the places in which you have influence?

. . . .

Bible in a year: Jonah 1,2; Revelation 10

Thursday 15 December
Jeremiah 50:1–28

Light on the horizon

PREPARE

'Lord, help me be still and quiet in your presence. I want to hear your voice. Amen.'

....

READ

Jeremiah 50:1–28

EXPLORE

Far from the Promised Land, the exiled Israelites live out their punishment in the ascendent Babylonian empire. With echoes of chapters 30 and 31, here is welcome reassurance from the Lord: 'When you turn back to me, you will be welcomed with joy. You will be able to come home, and I will avenge your oppressor,' (see vs 2–5). The tables will turn, and Babylon, once itself the great enemy from the north, will be crushed by a northern enemy of its own, leaving the way open for the Israelites to return to freedom.

While this message was spoken in a specific time and place to a particular group of people, there are ways it speaks to all of us. God alone is to be worshipped – sooner or later all false gods will be exposed as fraudulent pretenders and unrepentant worshippers condemned (v 2). Are you giving anything or anyone undue power, attention or influence over your life? God's purpose in punishment is for it to lead to repentance; he desires to forgive (v 20). What might God want to teach you from any adversity you are facing? God's plans will come to pass, and his promises will be fulfilled. Remind yourself of the bedrock of your heavenly father's faithfulness and love.

'They will ask the way to Zion and turn their faces towards it. They will come and bind themselves to the LORD in an everlasting covenant that will not be forgotten.'

Jeremiah 50:5

RESPOND

Thank God that he reigns over history, over world events, over *all*. He sees. He cares. His good purposes will come to pass.

....

Bible in a year: Jonah 3,4; Revelation 11

You and whose army?

PREPARE

'Lord, you are my strength, my rock, my high tower. I come to you for shelter and protection today. Amen.'

READ

Jeremiah 50:29-46

EXPLORE

As Jeremiah delivered this bold proclamation, Babylon was a superpower, an empire in its heyday, with Israel and Judah under its full control. As we read it centuries later, so many are still held captive by cruel and corrupt regimes, poverty, sickness, addiction, mental health battles, loneliness and more... 'Yet their Redeemer is strong; the LORD Almighty is his name' (v 34).

Jeremiah's first listeners would have understood the resonance and been reminded of another time their captors refused to let them go (Exodus 5-11). You can't underestimate the power of the Exodus story to build faith and trust in God and his ability to carry out audacious rescues. The God who had brought them out of slavery through parted waters would again deliver (Exodus 14:29-31). They could be confident of that.

These prophecies have sweeping scope, speaking of matters concerning nations and empires, armies and entire populations. This doesn't mean God isn't mindful of the relative minutiae of each of our lives, as Psalm 139 so beautifully reminds us. He knows us down to the very number of hairs on our heads (Luke 12:7). And with him on our side, there is nothing and no one we need fear.

'Like a lion ..., I will chase Babylon from its land in an instant ... Who is like me? And what shepherd can stand against me?'

Jeremiah 50:44

RESPOND

Ask God to give you eyes to see the spiritual reality of the battles you face, and give thanks for his protection.

Bible in a year: Micah 1-3; Psalm 144

Irredeemable

PREPARE

'You are the light that shines in the darkness, Jesus, and the darkness will never overcome you. Thank you for the gift of your life, death and resurrection. Amen.'

READ

Jeremiah 51:1–32

EXPLORE

How many pop songs can you think of which include some form of the sentiment, 'I'll never give up on you'? If we don't stop to give it much thought, we might well nod an inner assent to the principle. But sometimes, giving up is the right thing to do. It is right to leave an abusive relationship. It is right to amputate a septic limb. It is right to bring down a corrupt organisation.

God's people spend 70 years living in Babylon, seeking its good, endeavouring to influence its culture, demonstrating their faith (29:7), 'but she cannot be healed' (v 9). In fact, Babylon's evil has become so potent it has poisoned the whole world (v 7).

There are times in biblical history that, for the sake of his greater purposes for good, God enacted catastrophic judgement – on a vast number of wicked people in the time of Noah (Genesis 6), Sodom and Gomorrah (Genesis 19), and the Egyptian army (Exodus 14). This is God's earth, which he founded in wisdom and understanding (v 15). While there is hope for restoration and redemption, he withholds judgement. But sometimes there isn't (v 13).

> 'We would have healed Babylon, but she cannot be healed; let us leave her and each go to our own land, for her judgement reaches to the skies, it rises as high as the heavens.'
>
> **Jeremiah 51:9**

RESPOND

Are there any situations or relationships where the right thing to do is walk away? Ask God to give you courage to take hard decisions in pursuit of holiness.

Bible in a year: Micah 4,5; Revelation 12

Status check

PREPARE

'It is you alone who are to be feared, Lord. Help me to overcome my fear of others. Amen.'

··

READ

Psalm 76

EXPLORE

Today is my birthday. I bet you didn't know that! And of course, I'd only expect my immediate family to have it marked on their calendars. On the other hand, I imagine a good number of the singer Billie Eilish's 88 million followers on social media to be wishing her many happy returns today. This is going to connect to our psalm, I promise!

Psalm 76 may have struck you as a psalm about war and how warlike, fierce and angry God can get. But here's the thing: as we've seen in Jeremiah, these were rough and ready, bloody and brutal times in which the most respected were the fiercest warriors, leaders who defeated enemies in battle and defended their people and land. In reaching for picture language to express how far above and beyond the greatest humans on earth the Lord is, this was the obvious way for the psalm writer to go.

In many cultures today, a celebrity is esteemed more highly than an army general. But God's fame (v 1), influence (v 8) and radiance (v 4) are infinitely greater. And a week today, over two millennia after his birth, the birthday of Jesus, God incarnate, will be celebrated in every corner of the world.

You are radiant with light, more majestic than mountains rich with game.

Psalm 76:4

RESPOND

Compose your own psalm of praise. To what will you compare God's majesty, his status, his glory?

··

Bible in a year: Micah 6,7; Revelation 13

Monday 19 December
Jeremiah 51:33–64

The (much) bigger picture

PREPARE
Are you disheartened and depressed by all that is wrong in the world? Remind yourself that God *will* bring justice and make all things right.

....

READ
Jeremiah 51:33–64

EXPLORE
As Jonah was swallowed and vomited out by a large fish, so the exiles have experienced life as captives in the serpent Babylon (v 34). Biblical imagery is seldom chosen carelessly; the serpent has appeared before, as Satan in the garden of Eden (Genesis 3:1–15). And so, Babylon is meant to represent evil on a cosmic scale here (v 49).

Jeremiah's word from God on the matter of evil here gives three reasons to be hopeful. The first is that God hates it more than anyone, as you can see from the gory retribution lined up for Babylon (vs 36–44). The second is that God's people will be saved from the wreckage (vs 45,46). The third is that, under our true King, 'whose name is the Lord Almighty' (v 57), evil will one day come to an end: Babylon will 'sink to rise no more' (v 64).

It can feel like evil has free rein on earth and that there is no end in sight to the suffering of both people and planet. But there is a time coming when 'heaven and earth and all that is in them will shout for joy' (v 48). We just have to hold on with patience and faith.

> 'Then heaven and earth and all that is in them will shout for joy over Babylon.'
>
> **Jeremiah 51:48**

RESPOND
'Lord, I will wait for you. I will be strong and take heart, and I will wait for you. Amen.'

....

Bible in a year: Nahum 1–3; Revelation 14

His word, his bond

PREPARE

Talk to God about what these weeks in Jeremiah have been like for you, and ask him to show you if any of your perceptions of him are distortions.

• •

READ

Jeremiah 52:1–34

EXPLORE

Jeremiah's prophetic commission was through the word of God 'to uproot and tear down, to destroy and overthrow, to build and to plant' (1:10). As this last chapter comprehensively outlines, the uprooting, tearing down, destroying and overthrowing have come to pass. The city, the Temple and the royal palace have been razed to the ground. God has thrust his people from his presence in no uncertain terms. Uncomfortable as this may make us, consider the alternative: a deity who spouts empty words with no real-world impact. Who would respect, worship or obey such a god? A deity who doesn't care about evil, injustice or idolatry. Who could love or trust such a god?

I wonder if you have been to any carol services this year, and if so, whether you heard Isaiah 9 read? The promise of a child born to reign in peace for ever, establishing a kingdom of justice and righteousness; a light dawning, joy increasing, a time of great rejoicing and the end of the bloody warfare that continues to blight the earth today.

The baby was born. As to the rest, based on his track record, we can trust that 'the zeal of the Lord Almighty will accomplish this' (Isaiah 9:7).

> Of the greatness of his government and peace there will be no end...
>
> **Isaiah 9:7**

RESPOND

'Thank you, Father God, that your words have power, and that with your judgement comes mercy and forgiveness. Amen.'

• •

Bible in a year: Habakkuk 1–3; Psalm 145

REVEALING JESUS

Revealing Jesus is Scripture Union's mission framework, designed to help you journey into faith with the **95%** of children and young people not in church.

FIND OUT MORE: SU.ORG.UK/REVEALINGJESUS

Friends reunited

About the writer
Ro Willoughby

For many years, Ro was an editor with Scripture Union. She is now a lay minister at St Chad's Woodseats, Sheffield, engaging with people of all ages. Recently, for the first time in decades, she's bought a new Bible, just for herself. She is so delighted with its fresh layout and reference material.

One advantage of being a preacher's wife is that millions of his spoken words get recorded, or even videoed, for posterity. My husband died over four years ago. Occasionally, I turn on one of his sermons, not so much to listen to it, but just to hear his voice.

Having agreed to write for *Daily Bread*, I listened to a series of his lectures on Philippians, delivered in St Paul's Finchley, London, in 2011. This time I wanted to hear the content of the lectures, not listen to his voice. They have inspired and shaped these notes.

Paul was living under house arrest, probably in Rome, in the late 50s and early 60s. He sensed the end of his life was near but was as energetic as ever for the gospel. The whole palace guard (where elite soldiers and prisoners resided) had heard about him.

Philippi, in north-eastern Greece, was a Roman colony for discharged veteran soldiers. (The letter is full of military allusions.) He visited the city at least twice (Acts 16; 20:6), nurturing the embryonic faith of the socially diverse Philippian church. Among the first three converts were Lydia, a prayerful, wealthy Jewish immigrant widow, a local Greek slave girl and an official in the prison service.

Paul really loved these Christians. His appreciative personal letter reads as one man to his friends, urging them to be united and strong in faith when faced with opposition. Its powerful message remains so true today.

Wednesday 21 December
Philippians 1:1–11

Yearning for you

PREPARE
What do you think 'being confident' means? How confident are you in your Christian faith?

. . . .

READ
Philippians 1:1–11

EXPLORE
'I would never be brave enough to do anything like that!' Ever heard anyone express their lack of personal self-confidence? Some people may be confident of their abilities but may still be unsure how they might be received. Others lack confidence because they doubt the relevance or truth of what they have got to say.

Strikingly, the opening paragraphs of Paul's letter are brimming with confidence on every level. Look at how confident he is of the love the Philippian Christians have for him (vs 5,7,9). In response, he yearns for them (v 8). What about his own confidence in their faith and his right to support and advise them? And look at how confident he is in God and the gospel of Jesus Christ.

It is almost overwhelming. It reads so boldly. God was not asking them to be like Paul, but his example was there to be imitated. No need to feel intimidated. It was just that they experienced God's love through Paul's ministry. Here is a fabulous example of one Christian feeding the faith of others who know and trust each other.

And this is my prayer ... that you may be able to discern what is best and may be pure and blameless...

Philippians 1:9,10

RESPOND
How do you pray for those whose faith in God really matters to you? When you pray for them, is your prayer similar to Paul's prayer for the Philippians? How do you show your confidence in them and in God?

. . . .

Bible in a year: Zephaniah 1–3; Revelation 15

What matters most

PREPARE
Think of a time when something good emerged in your life out of something bad. Where was God in this?

READ
Philippians 1:12–18a

EXPLORE

Paul's house arrest meant that the good news became more widely known. He had a captive audience (v 13). He points out to the Philippians at least one other good thing that has happened (v 14). He even turns something potentially displeasing into a blessing.

He brushes off suspiciously motivated preachers (vs 15–18). He doesn't see them as serious opposition like those referred to later in the letter. Instead, he adopts Jesus' attitude in Mark 9:38–41: 'Whoever is not against us is for us.' What matters is that people hear about Jesus. Being united in Christ mattered to Paul. He emphasises this throughout his letter.

There are many Christian groupings throughout the wider church. Some revolve around a personality or history, a particular doctrine or emphasis, or a desire to reach a geographical area or section of society. Many result from a fall-out. Paul drew attention to what all Christians hold in common. Together we preach Christ crucified (1 Corinthians 1:23). It is the role of the Holy Spirit to then convict people of their need for God's forgiveness and love. Tertullian, the early church father, told how pagans commented on Christians' behaviour: 'See how they love one another.'

But what does it matter? The important thing is that in every way, whether from false motives or true, Christ is preached.
Philippians 1:18a

> ### RESPOND
> Pray for God to bring healing among Christians where there is bitter division, recognising that there are many ways to proclaim the good news.

Bible in a year: Haggai 1,2; Revelation 16

Friday 23 December
Philippians 1:18b–26

That bucket list!

PREPARE
'I'll praise my maker, while I have breath, and when my voice is lost in death, praise shall possess my noblest powers.'* Pause to reflect on this.

....

READ
Philippians 1:18b–26

EXPLORE
I once sat with a group of teenagers as they devised their own bucket list – not so much what they wanted to do before they died, but more of a wish list. Death was far from their minds. Unlike Paul! He knew his death day was close. What might he have placed on his bucket list?

For him it was a matter of doing what he had always done. He would continue to rejoice. He expects people to go on praying. He expects God to save him, whether this means 'saved from imprisonment' or 'saved to spend eternity with Christ' (v 19). He hopes, with confidence, to remain faithful to Christ, alive or dead. He will do his best for Christ while he has breath. Reflecting on his well-known words in verse 21, how is he able to say and mean them? He knows what he would prefer (v 23).

Of course, the choice is not his. Fully aware of his pending death, he was well prepared to be with Christ. In many parts of the world, where death is far more present in daily living, people grasp each day as a gift. In our society, that is not always the case. Even many Christians assume that their death is not anytime soon.

For to me, to live is Christ and to die is gain.
Philippians 1:21

RESPOND
Paul challenges us to take each day as a gift. How are you energetically serving Christ now, actively looking forward to your eternal destination?

*Jubilate Hymns gives the original first line: 'I'll praise my maker with my breath'. Isaac Watts (1674–1748)

....

Bible in a year: Zechariah 1,2; Psalms 146,147

Two-sided conversations

PREPARE
Peace on earth! How bothered are you that Christians fall out with each other?

∙∙

READ
Philippians 1:27 – 2:4

EXPLORE
It is unsatisfying to eavesdrop on an animated phone conversation and only hear half the story. Here we have Paul's side of a debate, but we don't know the exact details, nor his readers' response.

Something has gone wrong. There is opposition from outside. Paul urges these Christians to be like citizens, conducting themselves like soldiers – military images made sense in Philippi. They are to stand firm and strive together as though in battle (v 27). Paul empathises with them in their struggle.

This mattered because there was disunity within. Maybe Paul is referring to wrongly motivated preaching (1:15). Whatever, he reminds them of their fellowship in the past and what they still have in common (2:1–4). They are united with Christ. They belong to him and therefore belong to each other. He urges them to set their minds to rediscover what they share, seeking to love and value one another beyond themselves. Acquiescence is not enough. Cooperation and a spirit of unity is called for, even if they disagree.

On Christmas Eve, we are reminded that Jesus was born in a divided country. The Middle East is still riven by religious barriers. Pray for peace in that region.

> Do nothing out of selfish ambition or vain conceit. Rather, in humility value others above yourselves.

Philippians 2:3

RESPOND
Christians, finding themselves at odds with other Christians, may never hear the other side of the conversation. Pray that they will set their minds and hearts on sharing the same love, being in one spirit and one mind.

Bible in a year: Zechariah 3,4; Revelation 17

Sunday 25 December
Philippians 2:5–11

A servant prince

PREPARE
On Christmas Day, families enjoy their customary celebrations, often with few surprises. When did God last take you by surprise?

....

READ
Philippians 2:5–11

EXPLORE
Every Christmas Day we see pictures of the British royal family arriving at the church near Sandringham House in Norfolk. Imagine the surprise if one year a royal prince, dressed as the chauffeur, drove the car, jumped out to open the door for passengers, then drove away. 'What made him do that?' we might ask. 'This isn't what princes do! Is it a joke?'

There was nothing to joke about when Prince Jesus took on the role of a servant, 'being made in human likeness'. But it was a surprise! Reflect on what Philippians says about what Jesus gave up in coming to this earth (vs 6–8). Jesus didn't talk about being humble. He just was: the foot-washer, the sin-bearer! Paul intends to shake his readers into marvelling at Jesus' humility. He is challenging us about how we serve others.

Paul wants to do far more than that. The resurrection, ascension and exaltation are the completion of Jesus' calling. He is greater than every other human person, including Caesar, who was called Lord. Jesus is 'the Lord', acknowledging he has always been God (v 11). All nations will ultimately recognise him.

Nativity retellings emphasise the earthly dimension of Jesus' birth. Today, join with Paul in thinking about the parallel event of Jesus' exaltation.

God exalted him to the highest place.
Philippians 2:9

RESPOND
'Though an infant now we view him, he will fill his Father's throne, gather all the nations to him, every knee shall then bow down.'

*'Angels from the Realms of Glory', James Montgomery, 1771–1854

....

Bible in a year: Zechariah 5,6; Revelation 18

Starlight

PREPARE

As you read, remember a time when you were walking at night, maybe carol singing, with just a few lights or the moon to break into the darkness.

. . . .

READ
Philippians 2:12–18

EXPLORE

During the Covid-19 pandemic, we longed to be present with those we love but learned to communicate with them in different ways. Yet it is never quite the same as being there (v 12). Paul feels his absence from the Philippians. He thinks he may never see them again. His letter will have to suffice.

What is clear, as he develops this theme, is that he so longs for his readers to excel. It is not that he wants any praise, but, as any caring parent, he wants the joy of knowing they have done well. So, he urges them to cooperate with God to make a difference in the world. Grumbling could tarnish their impact, so they should stop it (vs 14,15) and hold confidently and boldly to the word of life, the truth in Christ.

Earlier in the chapter he included what is probably an ancient hymn to inspire the Philippians to have the mind of Christ (2:5–11). Now he invites them to imagine themselves as stars in the sky, shining in a 'warped' world. The best-known star story ever is the one about a star that led wise men to Christ the king. We, too, are called to shine the way to Christ by our blameless lives, but even more, by the presence of Christ within us (v 15).

... it is God who works in you to will and to act in order to fulfil his good purpose.

Philippians 2:13

RESPOND
Who will be caught in the beam of your starlight today? Pray for them.

. . . .

Bible in a year: Zechariah 7,8; Revelation 19

Tuesday 27 December

Philippians 2:19–30

My friends

PREPARE

What does it mean to you to be Christlike?

....

READ

Philippians 2:19–30

EXPLORE

Paul was undoubtedly a leader. But he was also a team player. From these verses, what can you discover about his friends and colleagues, Timothy and Epaphroditus? Note this letter was authored by Paul *and* Timothy, a co-servant of Christ Jesus (1:1).

Paul came across Timothy in Lystra (see Acts 16:1–5). He became one of Paul's closest partners in the gospel, with a father–son relationship (v 22). Paul sent him to build up the faith of various churches. His love for, and trust in, Timothy is palpable. He is confident the Philippians would welcome him back.

Meanwhile, Paul is sending Epaphroditus back home to Philippi, presumably from Rome. (See also 4:18.) Here is another unsung brave hero of the faith – a brother, a co-worker, a fellow soldier, a messenger (v 25). What do these accolades suggest? You might say Paul goes over the top in his praise... except Paul is not like that. He offers praise where praise is due. He offers advice or admonishment when that is needed. Maybe he is fearful Epaphroditus will get a cool welcome. Or maybe Paul sees in him an outstanding Christian to be imitated: one who has suffered; one who is not an obvious leader.

Welcome him [Epaphroditus] in the Lord with great joy, and honour people like him.

Philippians 2:29

RESPOND

Who are the Christians you admire for their Christlike qualities? How do you speak of them? How do you imitate them? Pray that God will enable them to remain Christlike.

....

Bible in a year: Zechariah 9,10; Psalm 148

Leaving the past behind

PREPARE
Look back at the people and places that have shaped your past.

. . . .

READ
Philippians 3:1–11

EXPLORE
I never once thought about the words of my nineteenth-century school song. Bizarrely, it was titled, 'All the past we leave behind'. Once a year, I gustily sang about taking up the task eternal, conquering, venturing, being a pioneer. In other words, forget about schooldays, looking boldly to the future.

Paul would never forget *his* heritage. As a Jew he was proud to belong to God's covenant people, Israel. He conscientiously kept the Law. He genuinely wanted to please God. But he came to realise this heritage was not enough. These Jewish opponents in Philippi who insisted that Christians should be circumcised have got it seriously wrong (v 2). That issue had already been settled in the Council of Jerusalem (Acts 15:5–11).

However, in comparison with knowing Christ, he describes his Jewish heritage as garbage, using a strong word (v 8).

To be gloriously 'found in Christ' means suffering and loss. It means knowing the power of Christ's resurrection, being raised to new life in death (vs 8,9). We sense that words fail him!

Our own backgrounds, schooldays and life experiences, good and bad, shape us. But in the light of the 'surpassing worth of knowing Christ Jesus our Lord', our past fades in its significance. Belonging to him shapes everything (v 8).

I want to know Christ – yes, to know the power of his resurrection and participation in his sufferings...

Philippians 3:10

RESPOND
Reflect on the events and influences that have made you who you are. How has Jesus Christ transformed you? Talk with God about this.

. . . .

Bible in a year: Zechariah 11,12; Revelation 20

Thursday 29 December

Philippians 3:12 – 4:1

Run the race

PREPARE
How do you picture life beyond death? Ask God to give you a greater sense of expectation.

READ
Philippians 3:12 – 4:1

EXPLORE
My husband died suddenly. But he ran the race with Christ right up to the finishing post. For him, it was all joy. For those who loved him, it has inevitably been bittersweet. As Paul acknowledged, we have not yet fully grasped what it means to keep on track with Christ, nor are we sufficiently like him. But we do have our eyes fixed on that eternal prize to claim our full heavenly citizenship. That is where we truly belong (v 14).

Paul urges the Christians in Philippi to keep a note of what they have already experienced and, like him, not look back (v 13). He invites them to choose some other Christlike role models. They cannot imitate him for long; his earthly life will soon be over (v 17). He emotionally warns them about false teachers among them, whom he speaks of as enemies of cross-shaped living. There are certainly bumps on the track, but we must keep pressing forward (4:1).

Paul is so eager to get to the finishing post that he is almost falling over himself. Once there, he will exist in the world with no conflict, where Christ is fully in control. His own physical body, and ours, will be transformed to be something like Jesus' glorious resurrection body (v 21).

> But our citizenship is in heaven. And we eagerly await a Saviour from there, the Lord Jesus Christ...
>
> **Philippians 3:20**

RESPOND
Take a deep breath! Have you begun to grasp what this will be like? Ask God to give you a fresh expectation of resurrection life beyond death.

Bible in a year: Zechariah 13,14; Revelation 21

Co-workers in disarray

PREPARE
What do you appreciate about other Christians in your church? How far do you feel you are in a team together?

....

READ
Philippians 4:2–9

EXPLORE
This morning, the sacking of the manager of a top internationally famous football team has been announced. The club is in serious disarray. It is painful for everyone, but especially for the squad of players.

The team in Philippi is in distress. Two faithful women in leadership have fallen out. Paul urges them to seek out what they have in common in Christ and to make their peace. What is more, he recognises that they need help from their co-workers. When there are disagreements among Christians, intervention needs to be made as early as possible. People will begin to take sides; differences will become irreconcilable and unity broken.

Paul confidently encourages his co-workers to learn from him (v 9). If peace between Christians exists, it is always apparent because their lives are on view to one another and to the whole world (v 5). Their lives are also open to God himself. Together, they are to find their joy in him. Tell God about everything, expect to be transformed, and together, experience his unifying peace and his very presence (vs 7,9). Paul emphasises, yet again, the importance of filling the mind with 'God-truth', a lifestyle habit.

Whatever you have learned or received or heard from me, or seen in me – put it into practice. And the God of peace will be with you.

Philippians 4:9

RESPOND
In verse 8, Paul suggests eight markers of God's presence and activity. Choose one of them. Identify when you have been aware of God's presence through this characteristic.

....

Bible in a year: Malachi 1,2; Psalms 149,150

Saturday 31 December
Philippians 4:10–23

Giving and receiving

PREPARE
Do you prefer to give to others or to receive from them? When it comes to God, which do you find easier, giving or receiving?

....

READ
Philippians 4:10–23

EXPLORE
Celebrities interviewed for a magazine are sometimes asked if they prefer to give or to receive, or neither or both. Paul would probably answer, 'Both!' He had given his life over to serving God and had given up everything for the sake of knowing Christ (3:8). Elsewhere, he wrote a list of his sufferings for the gospel (2 Corinthians 11:16–33). In particular, he has showered his love and affection upon these Christians.

For their part, they have a history of being generous towards him (v 16). Most recently, Epaphroditus has brought a gift from them to him in prison (v 18). How far do you think Paul is saying, 'I don't need anything! You needn't have bothered', or 'Thank you, I'm really grateful'? Again, both are probably true. Paul has learned to be content (v 11).

I grew up thinking verse 13 meant that I could do and be anything I want.

The sky is the limit. (I realised that was impossible.) Paul meant that he accepted whatever came his way in life because God's strength in him was inexhaustible.

We may be generous and grumble like the Philippians. But essentially, God calls us to be content, living a cross-shaped life, like Jesus. We receive far more than we give.

And my God will meet all your needs according to the riches of his glory in Christ Jesus.

Philippians 4:19

RESPOND
'May the ever-flowing grace of the Lord Jesus Christ, the inexhaustible generosity of God and the union with the Holy Spirit be with us all. Amen.'

....

Bible in a year: Malachi 3,4; Revelation 22